Dorothy Molter

The Root Beer Lady

by Sarah Guy-Levar and Terri Schocke

Adventure Publications, Inc.
Cambridge, MN

Acknowledgments

I'd like to thank the following: Peg Rosett, board member, tour guide and the greatest angel of them all, then and now. Butch Diesslin, Board President, steward, guide, mentor and friend. Bob Cotton, a Knife Lake legend, because you were there. Mike Tincher, graphic designer of T Designs, for helping us look good. Rod, Tootsie and Mike Loe of R&R Transfer for helping with the loads we can't handle. Grampa Phil Cady, the lead dog on the gangline. The museum Board of Directors, staff, volunteers and members, past and present. Loretta Molter, Dorothy's niece by marriage, for information and support. Steve Molter, Dorothy's great-nephew, for information and support. Bill Margis, Dorothy's great-nephew, for trusting us to acquire and preserve precious documents and photos of Dorothy's. Barb Cary-Hall, for her generous support and permission to use her father's work for the good of the museum. Jean and Jack Guy, my parents, for all their support. My sisters Gina, Beth, Jody, Michelle and their families, for being my greatest cheerleaders. Andy, Laura and Claire, for making it all worthwhile. Brett Ortler, my editor, for his creativity and sense of humor.—Sarah Guy-Levar

I wish to thank Dale Swenson of Swenson Photography of Braham, MN. His beautiful portrait of Dorothy Molter on page 92 hangs in the Museum for all to enjoy. Thanks to the summer staff for your superb contribution to the Museum as fun tour guides and coworkers. Peg Rosett, a great friend and coworker, who has always been a guiding light for me. The late Bob Cary, for his wonderful storytelling ability, I'm happy to have known him. Terry Schocke, my husband, (who shares my name . . . really!) and offers me constant encouragement. Thanks for the use of some of your photographs in this book. To my parents and siblings who have always encouraged me when I needed it. Thank you Melvin, Marcia, John, Vicki, Dad (& Mom, I miss you). You are the best!—Terri Schocke

Photo Credits by photographer and page number.
   Front cover photos: Bob Cary (main, bottom right), all other photos courtesy of the Dorothy Molter Museum
   Back cover photos: Dale Swenson/Swenson Photography, Braham, MN (top left), **Bob Cary** (bottom left), **Chris Bursch** (center right), all other photos courtesy of the Dorothy Molter Museum

   Dennis Berry: 31 (top), 32 (top), 62 (top) **Bob Cary**: 43 (top) **Dave and Laura Chelesnik**: 94 **Julie Hignell**: 38, 54, 67, 84 (all) **Sarah Guy Levar**: 70 (bottom) **Marlin Levison**: 92 (left), 151 **Steve Molter**: 79 **Peg Rosett**: 48 (top right), 58, 59, 71, 72, 81, 85, 86, 88, 92 (left) **Terri Schocke**: 15, 16 (all), 18, 19, 20, 22 (All), 23, 25, 33, 34, 35, 49 (top, middle), 70 (Top), 82, 83, 89 (top, middle, bottom), 113, 121, 144, 153 (top) **Dave Sebesta**: 15 (bottom) **Dale Swenson/ Swenson Photography, Braham, MN**: 92 (right) **Mike Tincher**: 89 (root beer), Maps on page 40, 90 courtesy of USDA Superior National Forest. All other photos courtesy of the Dorothy Molter Museum.

Edited by Brett Ortler

Book design by Jonathan Norberg

Cover design by Jonathan Norberg and Lora Westberg

10 9 8 7 6 5 4 3 2 1

Copyright 2011 by Sarah Guy-Levar and Terri Schocke
Published by Adventure Publications
820 Cleveland Street South
Cambridge, MN 55008
1-800-678-7006
www.adventurepublications.net

Table of Contents

Location of Dorothy Molter's Property

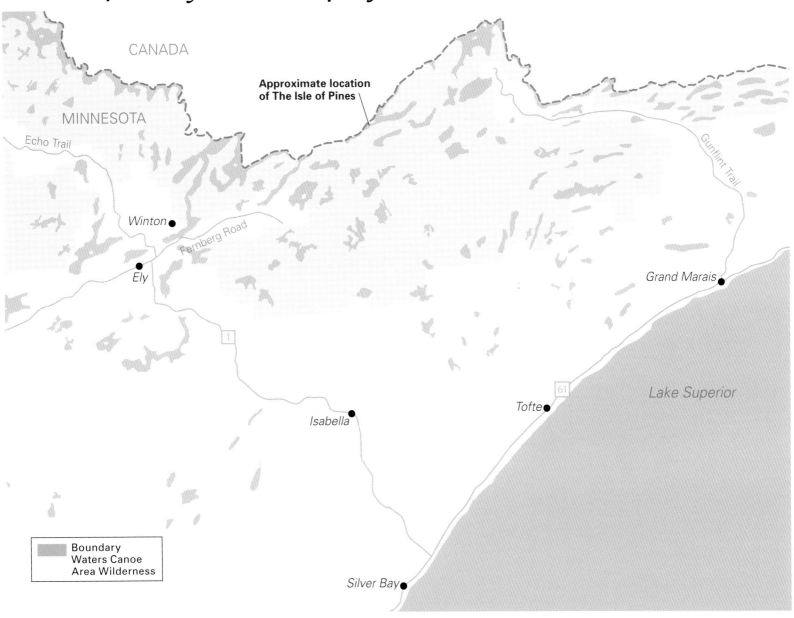

CANADA

MINNESOTA

Echo Trail

**Approximate location
of The Isle of Pines**

Gunflint Trail

Winton●

Fernberg Road

●
Ely

Grand Marais ●

1

61

Tofte●

Lake Superior

Isabella ●

Boundary
Waters Canoe
Area Wilderness

Silver Bay ●

Preface

It is not surprising that the lilacs still bloom on the Isle of Pines of Knife Lake. *Syringa vulgaris* can withstand the scorching heat of a ninety-degree summer day and the drought of a rainless August. This stalwart northland perennial endures the frigid temperatures of subzero winters. And yet, it still blossoms every spring to put forth it's small, fragrant flowers. This tough plant is not unlike the hero of our story. An unlikely transplant, Dorothy became the last legal resident of the Boundary Waters Canoe Area Wilderness.

The wilderness has a determined way of returning to itself. The cleared site of an old cabin allows the sun to warm the ground. The freezing and thawing of water creates cracks and crevices. Soil fills in, a seed gently lands. Untraveled paths disappear as alders encroach. Suddenly it starts to appear as if no one was ever there. Yet Dorothy's lilacs, with their deep roots and indomitable spirit, refuse to give up their strong hold. They, like her spirit, remain.

Introduction

Born in Pennsylvania and raised in Chicago, Dorothy would grow to become a legend of Minnesota's famed Boundary Waters Canoe Area (BWCA). For 56 years, she lived alone on the Isle of Pines on Knife Lake, 15 miles (and five portages) from the nearest road. When Dorothy died in 1986, she was the last remaining resident of the Boundary Waters Canoe Area. Life in the North Woods was rife with adversity; there were bears in the summer, canoe-swamping swells on the lakes, and of course, Minnesota's fierce winters, yet Dorothy managed to overcome—and even embrace—all challenges she faced.

The Nightingale of the North Woods

A licensed nurse, Dorothy first came to the Isle of Pines as a vacationer with her family in 1930. At that time, the Isle of Pines was a fishing resort. She visited again in 1931, and soon she became a regular visitor. Recognizing her toughness and her love for the North Woods, Bill Berglund, the owner of the resort, realized that Dorothy would be a perfect employee. Berglund's health was failing, so he offered her room and board in exchange for her nursing skills. More importantly, he promised to will the resort to Dorothy. After Bill's death, Dorothy was alone on the island. Dorothy's background in nursing made her an ideal first-responder, and she was often the only source of medical assistance for those in the area. Outfitters would often point her island out on the map and tell their clients, "If you run into trouble, head to Dorothy's." She assisted many tourists and residents, garnering her the nickname "The Nightingale of the North Woods."

The "Loneliest" Woman in America

Dorothy's isolation—and her status as a single woman in an area traditionally populated by men—eventually attracted attention. Dorothy received thousands of visitors over the years, including canoeists, tourists and anglers, reporters from national magazines, and even a movie star or two. Dorothy was first thrust into the national spotlight in 1952 when she was featured in a *Saturday Evening Post* article entitled "The Loneliest Woman in America." While the story depicted Dorothy in a positive light, Dorothy scoffed at the title, as she was hardly lonely. On the contrary, at times she had more company than she knew what to do with.

The Root Beer Lady

In what came to be called "the Knife Lake War," Dorothy was involved in a protracted legal fight with the government over her land, which the U.S. Forest Service wanted to set aside as a wilderness. Over the years, a number of travel restrictions were implemented, making it impossible for Dorothy to transport heavy goods, such as soda pop, to the resort. As Dorothy no longer could sell soft drinks for her visitors, she began making her own root beer, which she brewed using clean, clear Knife Lake water. This garnered her the name "the Root Beer Lady of Knife Lake." Dorothy's islands quickly became a wilderness destination and she received thousands of visitors each summer.

Dorothy's Legacy and the Dorothy Molter Museum

No matter why they visited, Dorothy's visitors were rarely disappointed, as she managed to live up to her reputation. She was friendly, loyal, good-natured, and, above all, kind. Evidence of this is found in the letters, journals and personal accounts that follow. When she passed away in 1986, Dorothy had long been a legend of the North Woods. The Dorothy Molter Museum was established in order to preserve Dorothy's legacy; it features Dorothy's root beer, extensive record of photographs, documents, and even the original buildings from the Isle of Pines, which were transported from the islands via sled dog teams, snowmobiles and all-terrain vehicles.

Dorothy's Story Today

In a world that is ever more technologically connected and where nature is almost an afterthought, stories like Dorothy's are rare and important, as they can show how one person can live—and thrive—despite all adversity. Dorothy Molter lived a remarkable life. This is her story.

I fell in love with the canoe country then and it's never lost its charm . . . It was like something out of Hiawatha.
—Dorothy quoted in Andrew Hamilton's, "The Loneliest Woman in America," *the Saturday Evening Post*, October 18, 1952

Her remote, hardy existence also attracted many journalists, and . . . the Saturday Evening Post called her "The Loneliest Woman in America." But during some years as many as 6,500 visitors had signed the guest book in her cabin, and in 1984 she told a reporter, "I've never been lonely in my life."—Dean Rebuffoni, *Minneapolis Star and Tribune*, December 19, 1986

With the leaves full and the summer scent in the air, I sometimes think about the last time I canoed the Boundary Waters out of Ely, Minn. Dorothy Molter still was on Knife Lake, five portages from town, 15 miles from the nearest road. I made the obligatory visit. Thousands of other paddlers each year did the same.

I remember the relief I felt while tying to the dock with the broken parking meter. It had been a hard day, punctuated by wearying portages, one at least a mile. I was in need of a rest.

I also remember my astonishment to learn that Dorothy had been through that very same lengthy portage in early spring, generously pushing aside deadfalls, preening her beloved wilderness for the hordes that would follow. She had turned 76.
—John Husar, "On Film: A Tribute to a Remarkable Woman," *Chicago Tribune*, May 22, 1988

To many paddlers, the Boundary Waters is all about lakes, loon calls, northern lights . . . and root beer. For 56 years, those who paddled deep into Minnesota's Boundary Waters Canoe Area Wilderness to the Isle of Pines shared a cold, homemade root beer with Dorothy Molter . . . better known as the "Root Beer Lady"—Jeff Rennicke, *Backpacker*, June 2001

DOROTHY'S EARLY YEARS

It was over one hundred years ago that Dorothy Molter's story began. Her life started in Arnold, Pennsylvania. Dorothy was the third of six children born to Mattie and John "Cap" Molter; she was born on May 6, 1907. In these photos you can see Dorothy and her siblings in a happier time. However when Dorothy was seven years of age, her beloved mother Mattie died. This was a huge blow to the family because their father Cap held a job with the Baltimore and Ohio Railroad and was seldom home long enough to care for the children on his own.

TOP LEFT: Dorothy and siblings (Dorothy is second from the left)

TOP RIGHT: A photo of Dorothy as a young student

BOTTOM LEFT: Dorothy in Chicago during junior high

BOTTOM RIGHT: Dorothy in a swing

A Tragic Loss

The only option available to Cap was to put his children in an orphanage in Cincinnati, Ohio. He was then able to visit them, as the railroad he worked for made regular stops there. The children remained in the orphanage as a family group for five years. The family was reunited in 1919 when Cap married his second wife, Myrtle Leist from Circleville, Ohio.

Cap, Myrtle and the six children moved to northern Indiana as a family. The Molters moved again and resettled in Chicago, Illinois. An excellent student, Dorothy continued her education at Calumet High School, where she was active in tennis, basketball and swimming and was a member of the school's rifle team. She excelled at marksmanship; in 1925, she was the Champion Marksman in the girl's division of Chicago's citywide competition, which was held at the Old Chicago Coliseum. Little did she know that her shooting skills would serve her well later in life when she was chasing off a belligerent bear or bagging a deer for venison stew.

Following high school graduation, Dorothy pursued a nursing career by enrolling for training at Auburn Park Hospital.

TOP LEFT: Dorothy's high school graduation photo

TOP RIGHT: Dorothy's graduating class at nursing school (Dorothy is in the front row, third from the left)

BOTTOM: Dorothy's nursing school graduation photo

In 1929, Dorothy's father, Cap (short for captain), was drawn to Basswood Lake, near Ely, in the hopes of catching a trophy northern pike. On May 16th of that year, a 45-pound, 12-ounce northern pike had been caught on Basswood Lake, setting a new state record. At that time Basswood Lake was famous for its many luxury resorts, unequaled fishing, and sightseeing tours that took place in excursion boats capable of holding 50 people. Even though Ely was remote, it was surprisingly accessible. In just one long day visitors could easily board the passenger train in Chicago and end up at the depot in Ely. Cap worked for the railroad, and railroad employees often had the benefit of riding for a reduced rate or even for free.

Dorothy's First Visits to the North Woods

It was while fishing on Basswood Lake that Cap learned of The Isle of Pines Resort, a rustic three-island fishing resort located further to the east on Knife Lake. This resort was more remote and in a sparsely populated area that was accessible only by canoe or floatplane. Knife Lake offered the trifecta of fishing—there were lunker northern pike, walleyes, and the elusive but highly sought-after lake trout. In addition to fishing, the lake possessed stunning beauty—high cliffs, crystal-clear water, unique rock formations, and stands of giant old-growth pines lining the shores. Cap booked a trip the following summer, and planned to bring along his wife Myrtle, his brother Bill, and two friends from the railroad. At the last minute one friend was unable to join them. Since Dorothy had just finished a semester of school, she was available to go with them in his place.

TOP: Dorothy and Bill Berglund in a hammock

CENTER: Dorothy during her youthful "Indian" phase

BOTTOM: Dorothy and Nebs on the Isle of Pines

Excerpts from Dorothy's Vacation Journals
DOROTHY'S FIRST VISIT, 1930

The trip to Isle of Pines was Dorothy's first visit to a wilderness area. As she was a city girl, this turned out to be quite an adventure. To truly understand what life was like in the area in the 1930s, it's best to let Dorothy do the talking. Thankfully, during her first two visits to the Isle of Pines, Dorothy kept vacation diaries; in them, it's clear how much she was in awe of the beauty, peace and serenity that this land of lakes offered.

Isle of Pines
Our camp is situated on the largest of three small islands. The two smaller islands are connected with the larger one by means of several logs which serve as bridges. The smaller islands are about the size of a tennis court. The larger one is about the size of a city block or less. On one of the small islands the caretaker has his camp. On the other small island is a one-bedroom cabin with a screen porch. On the large island is our cabin. Besides our cabin, another cabin occupies the other side of the island. But this cabin does not get as nice a view as we got from ours. Behind this cabin, the caretaker is building a one-room cabin for himself. Other small buildings on the island include kennels for the huskies for winter use, the icehouse, tool shacks, and last, but not least, there is "Old Faithful"—the ever welcome backhouse—nature's own.

TOP RIGHT: Winter Cabin

TOP LEFT: Nebs, Bill and Dorothy

BOTTOM LEFT: Bill teaches Dorothy to portage

BOTTOM RIGHT: Dorothy with a nearly 30-pound lake trout

Point Cabin

The island is well sheltered by timber which includes birch trees and all members of the fir tree. The island is also covered with wild flowers, ferns, wild berries, etc. There is very little grass, but lots of deer moss. The trees grow right off of the stones and rock. The island is rather hilly and is elevated above the level of the lake. Water snakes are rather numerous after storms. The remains of a porcupine lie in a secluded spot in the center of the island. The dock at the Geenans' Cabin is a good place to get minnows. A long log extends out into the lake and serves for several good purposes, and is a great aid to anyone seining for minnows or looking for a diving spot. The scenery there is pretty, but you can't enjoy it from the cabin as it is too far back from the shore and among the trees. I like our cabin best. Our cabin is built of logs. It has two bedrooms and one large room which serve as kitchen-dining room and parlor, etc. There is also a screen porch on which there on which there is a cot at one end and a table-stand at the other end. The porch has awnings over the windows, but they do not help much on windy days as there is no way to keep them down except by nailing them. Never-the-less, the porch made a good place to sleep. Each bedroom was furnished with a bed made from logs, and the beds proved to be very "comfy." There were old-time pictures on the walls. Nails in the walls furnished good hat racks and hangers.

It is situated directly off the lake and in plain view from the water. From this cabin you get the full benefit of the sunrise, sunset, moonrise, and a wider view of the country. Also you can see every boat or canoe which either comes in from or goes out to the portage. Almost directly in front of the cabin is the dock. It is a good landing place and also served well for a diving board. It could do nice tricks too—such as getting shaky and causing a fellow to fall in the lake if he wasn't careful. The lower side was also slippery too and that added to the excitement of the audience if anyone should step there unawares. Standing on the end of the dock you could see the bottom of the lake for nearly ten feet down as the water was very clear. It was exceptionally good water to drink.

TOP: Point Cabin

MIDDLE: Dorothy starting out near Moose Lake landing

BOTTOM: The Fishing Party—Cap, Myrtle, Dorothy, Uncle Bill (Cap's brother) and R.E. "Bob" Pyle, Cap's friend

Excerpts from Dorothy's Vacation Journals
DOROTHY'S FIRST VISIT, 1930 (continued)

A Long Way from "Civilization"

Occasionally we see a few campers but they usually camp
for the night and travel on the following day. There are very
pretty camp sites on the islands. Some campers traveled long
after dark. Our camp—not only being so far away from any
town—is also far from any type of communication. The only
way to correspond with the "outside world" is to write letters
and lay them aside until you see some camper going into town,
maybe a week later, more or less. Then the news becomes stale.
There is no way to get the latest news except from campers
who probably had heard the news several weeks previously.
Of course sometimes someone comes in direct from town and
you manage to get the very latest. Never-the-less, news of the
outside world is the least of your worries except when the news
comes directly from family or friends.

TOP: Bill Berglund assists a guest with a stringer of freshly caught fish

BOTTOM: Dorothy and Myrt between Ottertrack and Swamp Lakes
on Monument Portage, standing near the large steel international
boundary marker

Isle of Pines Nightlife

During the day the lake was sometimes rough, but at night, in fair weather, it was smooth as glass and occasionally you could hear a fish break water. When darkness fell everything was so quiet you could distinguish noises from across the lakes on the mainland. Occasionally the loon broke the silence. One night while watching the northern lights we heard several wolves. We also heard another sound which was probably made by a deer which the wolves were after. The northern lights were certainly pretty. They were different every night. They were white in color—except the last night we saw them, they were tinted pale green and pink. They usually form an arc in the sky to the north and the rays of light travel from west to east and visa versa. They beam way out across the sky and take on various forms and motion. One night they appeared to form separate descriptions and some rays seemed to form a long beaded lamp shade for the stars.

TOP: A gray wolf

BOTTOM: The northern lights (aurora borealis)

Excerpts from Dorothy's Vacation Journals
DOROTHY'S SECOND VISIT, 1931

Dorothy's Second Trip to the Isle of Pines

Dorothy visited the resort a second time in 1931. On that trip a new tradition was started. Each visitor's name and the dates they visited the resort were recorded on a small square piece of birch bark. These birch bark records show that Dorothy began to visit the resort for longer and longer stays. Initially, Dorothy was simply a tourist, but as she visited the resort more and more, she became a regular, and eventually, a resident. Dorothy's vacation journals from her second trip provide a vivid picture of life at the resort, and they show her becoming more and more comfortable in the north.

TOP: The popular common loon was named Minnesota's state bird

BOTTOM RIGHT: Although the beaver spends winters in a den, it is often visible in early spring, when ice begins to leave the lakes

BOTTOM LEFT: The male pine grosbeak, a year-round resident, is a colorful sight in the winter

A Typical Day at the Resort, Wednesday, August 19, 1931

Everyone up at 7:00 A.M. Had pancakes for breakfast as per usual and after that we went fishing. Mother stayed at the cabin; as she didn't care to go fishing. We fished all morning but had no luck. Bob and I explored the island and mainland. We climbed as high as we could possibly get and enjoyed the scenery very much. We could see Portage Lake, Vera Lake and Knife Lake, and further than the "Twin Islands," all in one birds eye view. We could see for miles around, the sky was pretty with numerous white clouds. While exploring through the trees and brush we saw many signs of deer, and what we thought might be the sign of a bear. But signs were as near as we got to seeing the real sight. We all met at the island and went in the cabin and had dinner. Afterwards, the men played poker until about 4 P.M., then we went fishing again—that is, Dad, Mother and I went. We had several bites but not much of a catch. I landed a great northern but threw it back. Another time I nearly landed a walleye, but it got away. Anyhow I had a good look at it. Well, better luck will come. We came home about dark then had supper. After supper we had quite a storm. The wind sure can blow up here. The rain came in on my cot so we had to move it inside. The wind sure did howl. In fact it was an ideal night for a "mystery thriller story." By bedtime the storm was over so we put the cot back on the porch. It cleared up nice after that and gave us the feeling that the fish would bite tomorrow. Of course the usual poker games went on this evening and when the wind died down the noise from the card game turned out to be just as loud if not louder—and that's saying something too. That ended another perfect day.

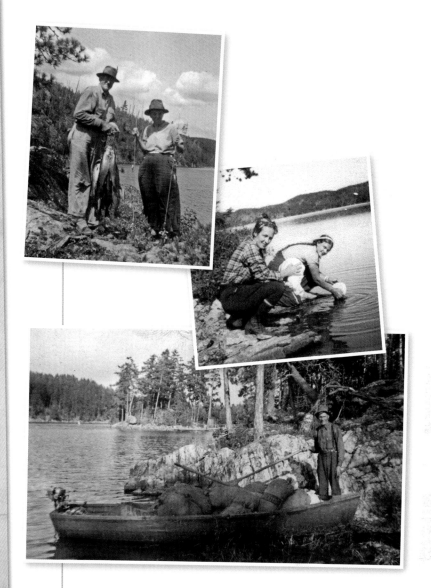

TOP: Cap and Myrtle with a stringer of fish

MIDDLE: Cleaning up lakeside after supper

BOTTOM: Bill Berglund transporting packs by boat

Excerpts from Dorothy's Vacation Journals

DOROTHY'S SECOND VISIT, 1931 (continued)

Fishing with the Rangers, Thursday, August 20, 1931

Got up this A.M. about 7:30, had breakfast and after camp chores were done, I went to the portage with Dad, Mother, Bob and Uncle Bill to catch minnows. We got several nice ones with the net. I took one end and Uncle Bill took the other end and we waded in the lake as deep as we could stand upright. After several attempts we got a nice mess of minnows. We also took pictures while passing the time seining for minnows. While we were there we met up with 2 game wardens and they helped us get more minnows. Finally about noontime we came back to the cabin for lunch, but after our boat was docked, one of the rangers caught a "walleye" with a minnow so all of us fishermen got the fever and forgot about lunch and went fishing. We fished for a couple of hours and between [the] Geenans, the rangers, and our party we got about 18 fish. I caught one 3-pound walleye and one 2-inch perch. Watta' catch. Ha Ha. We finally decided to come in to supper so we had fish, beans, biscuits, and other camp luxuries including lemon cream pie. The two rangers ate supper with us. After supper we went fishing again. Bob caught one walleye, I caught two, Uncle Bill caught two and the Geenans caught four. Then it was too dark to fish so back to the cabin we went. I wrote letters to John, Ruth and bunch and to Grandma. [The] Geenans are getting ready to go home tomorrow so Dad, Mother and Uncle Bill went over there tonight. There is just Bob and I at the cabin now so I guess we will play "Rummy" to pass the time away. This has been a good day. I sure love this country.

A North Woods Sunset Friday, August 21, 1931

There was a pretty sunset tonight. The Northern Lights were unusually pretty tonight. They lit up the sky so nice and it looked like Jack-o-lanterns or icicles hanging down from the stars.

ABOVE: A sunset in the North Woods

News from Knife Lake, Sunday August 23, 1931

Other news events and exciting moments of the day are:

1. Dad took a few pictures, also took two of the lightning early this A.M.

2. I went swimming for about a half hour.

3. Dad and Mother gave Fred some fish.

4. Bob went wading. (And How!)

5. Dad and I went log rolling also. (And How!)

6. Last, but not least—Uncle Willie's unusual ways of living made him quite a go-getter when we went for minnows.

7. Also Mother killed a snake, so I guess, we all earned tin medals. Did not see very many parties coming from the portage today. End of a perfect day. Dad, Mother and Uncle Bill saw a porcupine tonight.

ABOVE: A calm day with a lake view as smooth as glass

Excerpts from Dorothy's Vacation Journals
DOROTHY'S SECOND VISIT, 1931 (continued)

Palisades and Photographs, Monday, August 24, 1931

Got up about 7 A.M. The usual breakfast of pancakes we changed to cornmeal cakes which proved to be just as good, due of course, to Uncle Willie's good cooking. After breakfast we bummed around a bit, then all of the gang except Mother played "Michigan Rummy" until noon time. After that we decided to go across the bay and hike over the hills and get the lowdown on the scenery. So there we went, the whole gang. We sure climbed the hills and dashed through the thickets like a flock of wild animals. The scenery from the hilltops sure was pretty. We could see for miles around, in all directions. We could see several portages, Lake Vera, Twin Islands, our cabins, etc. It sure was worth while to climb up there to view the scenery . . . Then Dad and I took a few pictures, which I hope will turn out nice, as I'd sure like to keep those views . . . The sunset sure was pretty this evening. The moon also is very bright and shines on the lake like a mirror.

ABOVE: The Twin Islands as photographed from Thunder Point, where the north and south arms split on Knife Lake

Leaving the Lake, Saturday, August 29, 1931

Boy—Watta' day this was—I sure never will forget it and I wouldn't have missed it for the world. At about 7:30 Bill Berglund and Fred's helper came over to take us on our "watery journey" as far as several portages. We all hated to leave, but it had to be. We even bid Nebs (the dog) good-bye. We had a little trouble with the motor but after a half hour we were on our way. The lake was pretty rough. We had not gone very far when it began to rain and it rained most of the way out. It not only rained, it just poured down. At the lift-overs we had to make two trips. Mother, Dad and I stayed in the boat with Bill Berglund, while Uncle Bill and Bob came in the canoe with Fred's helper. At one of the portages, Bob and Uncle Bill saw a bear and two little cubs. At one of the lift-overs—Dad, Mother and I saw a doe and a fawn. It sure was a pretty sight and there was a pretty background, too. At one place, instead of going over to the next lake in the boat, we walked the mainland over a deer trail; here we saw the remains of a deer that had been eaten by wolves. It was a rather pitiful sight (if you look at it the way I do) . . . We had a little trouble getting the last portage but we all made the best of it except Berglund and Seely who had to argue and fight about our transportation. But once we got on the big lake we "scrammed" from one lake into another. Bob was a little out of sorts as he was afraid we would miss the train. It sure did pour down rain and the good old lakes were considerably rough . . . All had raincoats on, but that only partly protected us. The rain and the splashes from the waves had a good time rolling down our necks. Well, we all laughed and made merry and enjoyed the weather regardless. Dad took a few snap shots when opportunity permitted. We finally landed on the good old shore—all dripping wet, but not the least put out about it. There we carried our luggage to the top of the hill and tossed it into the "Winton Trading Co." truck and hopped in the truck . . . Mother sat in front with Mr. Seely and the rest of us sat in the back, that is, we sat when the truck didn't hit a bump and make us bounce around like a rubber ball. Dad tried to get snapshots, but he bounced around so much from the jolts of the truck that he only succeeded in getting one. Uncle Bill was sitting on a box. All of a sudden the truck

continued on page 22

Excerpts from Dorothy's Vacation Journals
DOROTHY'S SECOND VISIT, 1931 (continued)

went over a rock or an elephant (I don't know which) but Uncle Willie lost his throne and bounced up about a couple of feet and came down on the box with his 250 pounds. Well, the box crashed and it hit the floor of the truck about the same time he did. Well, he stands the box on the other side and sits on it and piles a couple of leather cushions on it and then sits down to enjoy solid comfort. Well, all is well when about ten minutes later the same thing happens . . . We should have saved the remains of the box for toothpicks, but we had enough junk to take home with us . . . Well, we got to Winton without mishap and just in the nick of time "for we could hear the train coming." Dad, Mother and Bob went home on the train. Uncle Bill and I per auto as we came. It was a bad morning to be out on the lake and the first part of our journey was pretty rough but we all laughed, joked and had a good time. In fact, we had a better time than we would have had if the sun had been shining all morning. I sure wouldn't have missed this last day for the world.

Well, this sure is the end of a real Perfect Day.

TOP: A mallard hen and ducklings

BOTTOM: A common loon

ABOVE: Shortly after Dorothy's second visit the autumn leaves
started to turn; one can only imagine her delight in this
change once she began to extend her stay through the fall

About Bill Berglund

During Dorothy's repeated visits to the north, she befriended Bill Berglund, the owner and operator of the resort. Berglund would play a central role in Dorothy's life and any telling of Dorothy's story requires a bit of background about Bill. The original owner of the Isle of Pines Resort, Bill acquired the islands from an official of the Swallow and Hopkins Lumber Company in 1925. He paid $350 for the three islands, which totaled ten acres.

One of three children, Bill was born to hard-working Swedish immigrants in New London, Minnesota, on August 4, 1874. Not much else is known about his early life other than that he was married and that he suffered a tragedy as a young man. His wife Ellen was a victim of the infamous Spanish Flu epidemic of 1918. Turning to the North Woods for solace, Bill followed the logging companies looking for work, eventually ending up in Winton, MN. In 1898, the Swallow and Hopkins Lumber Company had built a four-mile-long logging railroad from the shores of Fall Lake near Winton to Basswood Lake near the Canadian border. Railcars carried logs out to the sawmills, but to reach the mills the trains first had to cross a series of waterways formed by low log dams. Bill worked as a timber cutter for the company in the winter and also at the sawmill in Winton.

ABOVE: Bill and Nebs

A New Vocation

By the late 1910s the great virgin forests of red and white pine were depleted and the logging era was coming to a close. Work in the woods and sawmill in Winton was often quite sporadic so Bill guided trips into the wilderness at every chance he got. One of his customers was Jim O'Niel, a prospector in his eighties who wanted one last look at the old cedar log cabin he had spent so much time at 40 years before.

It was during the excursion to O'Niel's cabin that Bill Berglund became acquainted with Charles Ira Cook Jr. The two parties met on a portage and struck up a conversation; they eventually decided to camp together. During their shared meal Bill learned that Charles had a desire to explore more of the border country, fish and try his hand at trapping. Bill offered to partner up with Cook for the upcoming season, as he too wanted to see more of the big lakes and scout some of the trapping country. According to Charles' book *Trapping the Boundary Waters*, Charles was unsure of partnering with Bill, as he'd just met him, so he looked for a character reference before agreeing to spend a considerable amount of time in the bush with him. He turned to Leo Chosa, a future friend of Dorothy's and a mixed-blood American Indian who ran a trading post at Prairie Portage, located between Sucker and Basswood Lakes. When asked to describe Berglund, he said, "He's the orneriest bullheaded Swede that ever lived. The devil himself couldn't get along with him unless he had his own way all the time."

ABOVE: Logged forests recover with time; it is surprising how the shallow roots take hold and trees grow among the rocks

Hunting, Trapping and Fishing

Despite Chosa's less than resounding reference, Cook learned that Bill was honest and well thought of in the community, even though everyone considered him an incurable introvert. Over the course of the summer and fall of 1919 and the winter of 1920, Bill taught Charles everything he knew about camping, portaging, scouting, cooking, fishing, hunting and trapping. The duo covered hundreds of miles on the water and over portages; they traveled from the shores of Fall Lake (near Winton) to the easternmost lakes of the Minnesota-Canada border.

Winter in Minnesota can be long and tests even the strongest of characters. Bill and Charles eventually went their separate ways, apparently because of a dispute in which Bill accused Charles of trapping too early (when beaver pelts were not quite yet in their prime). By this time, folks had begun to acknowledge Bill's expertise as a woodsman, and his ability to travel quickly through canoe country became well known. This drew the attention of Winton game wardens Bill Hansen and John Linklater. Based out of the old fish and game headquarters in Winton, these wardens patrolled the Superior Game Refuge by dogsled. The refuge had been created in an attempt to protect the threatened moose and caribou populations. The wardens hired Bill to travel the area by snowshoe looking for trappers taking illegal furs. Traveling fifteen to twenty miles in a day was not uncommon.

ABOVE: Early Superior Game Refuge tent camp

While working as a warden, Bill became aware that a piece of property with three islands was available on Knife Lake, one of the lakes he considered among the prettiest in the refuge. By 1922, the forests of northeastern Minnesota were accessible by automobile or passenger train service right into Ely. Bill realized there was an increasing market for rustic fishing vacations and he capitalized on this by purchasing the islands. Using logs from the islands and the nearby mainland, he built two very basic two-bedroom cabins and rented them out by the week to anglers from all over the Midwest, who were eager to tap into the pristine fishing waters of the game refuge. Income from the resort did not cover all of Bill's expenses, so in the winter he moved to Winton, rented a room, and continued to trap and work for the wardens doing patrols of the refuge.

Dorothy Arrives to Help Out

At 57 years of age, Bill was essentially running a rustic wilderness resort by himself and working another job to boot. He needed help, but his introverted nature meant he didn't get along well with everyone. Luckily, his personality was a perfect platonic match for a shy young woman from Chicago. As Dorothy's family continued to vacation at the Isle of Pines, Bill realized what an asset she could be. Over the course of four years he watched her enthusiastically take on the chores of running a wilderness resort. Dorothy cleaned cabins, hauled ice to fill the iceboxes in the guest cabins, she helped stock up wood for the winter, and she even guided the occasional fishing party when the regular guides were booked.

TOP: Bill poses with resort guests back from a successful outing

BOTTOM: A young Dorothy was a perfect fit at the Isle of Pines Resort

An Offer of a Lifetime

By 1934, Dorothy was a member of the staff as much as she was a vacationer. Financially, times were tough. To keep the resort afloat, Bill worked in town. He also was overwhelmed with the everyday tasks of running the resort. All this took its toll on Bill's health, and he realized that he needed a nurse to help care for him. Dorothy was the perfect woman for the job, so Bill made Dorothy an offer she couldn't refuse. He offered her the opportunity to live year-round on Knife Lake. In return, she'd receive room and board, along with the benefit of staying in her beloved North Woods. He also promised that in exchange for her labor and medical assistance, the Isle of Pines would one day become hers.

Leaving Chicago for Good

Dorothy's decision wasn't very difficult to make. Aside from her love of the North Woods, there were other factors to consider. In 1934, the country was in the middle of the Great Depression. At that time Chicago was a town largely run by gangsters. Prohibition and bootlegging had brought violence into the north-side neighborhoods of Chicago. While Dorothy had graduated from nursing school, jobs were rare. She readily accepted Bill's proposal.

TOP: Dorothy experiences a Minnesota winter

BOTTOM: Dorothy learns how to snowshoe

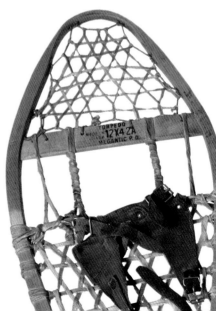

Dorothy received a great deal in return for her help. All of Bill's experience as a woodsman made him a skilled and proficient mentor. Under his tutelage she learned to hunt deer, trek the country on snowshoes, and track a myriad of animals based on the signs they left on the trees, snow and ground.

Life on the Lake

Once Dorothy moved up to stay in 1934, parts of the winter were spent in a rented room in town and other parts were spent "up at the lake." Frequent visitors from Bill's early days in Winton provided ample entertainment. Forest Service employees, game wardens, bush pilots, trappers and campers all convened at the Isle of Pines for one occasion or another. Bill enjoyed gathering with these visitors to play poker, smoke, drink and "shoot the bull." The tales of old trappers, outlaws, tragic events, and ghost stories were all enthralling to Dorothy, but when the language became too coarse Bill reminded her that she should probably dismiss herself and head for her bunk.

ABOVE: Prior to the invention of the snowmobile, Dorothy had to snowshoe to town during the winter

The Challenges of Everyday Life

Operating a four-cabin fishing resort in the wilderness certainly had its challenges. As there was no running water, water for cooking, drinking and washing up had to be hauled up from the lake. As there were no washers or dryers, laundry was also a challenge. This was especially true on cabin turnover day, when guests left and others arrived. This required a lot of cleaning and laundry in a short time. First, the cabin beds were stripped, and the sheets were soaked overnight in a copper boiler of hot water and soap. As there was no electricity (and no electric dryer), sheets were wrung by hand then hung to dry. Hanging them required strong hands and an even stronger back. Sheets hung until they were dry, perhaps two or even three days, depending on the weather. Towels were washed in a similar fashion, with a good scrubbing on a washboard to complete the job. Only later, when she was older, did Dorothy have a washing machine. It was gasoline powered, with a roller wringer, and she kept it down by the shoreline. One fisherman friend recalled a time when he was traveling on the lake on an early foggy morning—the only thing that guided him back to the island was the loud racket of that washing machine motor.

Hauling Ice

Hauling ice was another laborious chore. Ice blocks were hauled from the icehouse to the guest cabins for use in iceboxes, as there was no other refrigeration. These ice blocks were harvested from the lake in the winter. The ice was then hauled to the icehouse and stacked using sawdust and moss as insulation between the layers. When stored this way, the ice lasted through the summer. Guests used the ice to keep freshly caught fish cold and to cool beverages, so it wasn't a surprise to occasionally find a small piece of moss floating in your evening cocktail. If guests had a large catch of fish that wouldn't fit in the icebox, they would store them in a burlap sack, which were then strategically placed amid the ice blocks in the main icehouse. These sacks were crudely labeled with the fisherman's name—a stick was poked into the bag and attached with twine. On more than one occasion a sack of fish was forgotten and lost among the crevasses that were covered with layers of moss and sawdust. According to Bob Cotton, a dear friend of Dorothy's, cleaning out those sacks in late summer was the dirtiest job of all at the resort!

ABOVE: The many stages of the ice harvest, a process which was repeated every winter

Keeping the Home Fires Burning

"Bucking up wood" for the winter was also an ongoing project, and a lot of work. Ample supplies of firewood were available from the nearby islands and mainland, but producing it took a good deal of effort and time. The wood had to be located, sawed by hand, loaded into the canoe or boat, unloaded at the island, and then sawed into stove lengths, split and stacked. Dorothy would certainly have agreed with the old adage, "Wood warms you twice, once while putting it up and once while it burns."

Different types of wood were needed for particular tasks. Small pieces of cedar burn easily and hot, and are perfect for kindling and starting a fire. Aspen and birch burn quickly and warmed up the cabins in a hurry. Harder woods like maple and scrub oak provided a slow burn, keeping the stove going through the long, cold nights. In the summer, firewood was only used for the occasional campfire. Nevertheless, in the shoulder seasons of spring and fall, visitors would often keep a fire in the stove to stave off the chilly night temperatures, which sometimes fell into the thirties.

TOP: An old barrel stove kept the Point Cabin warm

BOTTOM: Dorothy cleans a fish in front of the cords of wood needed for the upcoming winter

Keeping Up the Place

Maintenance was an ongoing task. Strong winds and heavy snowstorms made a continual mess of the trails between the cabins, and fallen trees and branches had to be cleared away. Because the water levels varied in each season, the wooden footbridges connecting the islands needed periodic repairs. Other problems occasionally arose too: cabin roofs would leak, a porch's foundation would crumble, boats or canoes sprung leaks, or outboard motors would fail to start.

The Trading Post

Running the resort's "trading post" was another of Dorothy's duties. When floatplanes brought in supplies, guests and travelers could buy soda pop in glass bottles, candy bars, gasoline and other staples. As Dorothy never felt very comfortable making a big profit on these items, she sold the items at a small margin above what it cost to buy them and transport them to the island.

TOP: Footbridge from the Big Island to the Cady Cabin island

BOTTOM: Footbridge cribbing needed constant repair

The Resort in the Offseason

In the resort's offseason, Dorothy learned how to live off of the land. This was quite important, as it was instrumental to store a supply of meat in the fall for the coming winter. Bill's experience as a woodsman came in handy, and he taught Dorothy to recognize signs that deer were present, including where to look for antler scrapes or rubs and how to identify deer tracks and scat. All of these skills helped Dorothy become an efficient hunter, helping her bag the animal she needed to keep a pot of venison stew on the stove.

Of course, since there was no refrigeration at the resort, preserving venison took some effort. This work often occurred during the cool November weather. After a deer was shot, it was field dressed, hung up to dry, and cured with salt. Special cuts (like the loin) were eaten right away, while some of the less desirable cuts would be made into sausage, or were smoked to preserve them. Most of the time deer were hunted, as moose were protected during those early years and couldn't be hunted. Occasionally, Native Americans would take a moose and share it with their neighbors at the Isle of Pines. It wouldn't be unusual to learn that the stew you were eating might have some "Canadian beef" in it. Most game wardens looked the other way at these violations, as they were simply a way for poor families to put food on the table. Not many people ate beaver or bear, but some people in the bush would do so if they became hungry enough.

ABOVE: White-tailed deer

Ducks and Geese

Deer weren't the only wild game available in the fall, however. Hunting opportunities often presented themselves. A long hike over a portage might flush out a covey of ruffed grouse, while a paddle into a small lake might lead you to a flock of waterfowl. Such encounters often led to a nice dinner of roast duck or goose, perhaps served on a bed of locally gathered wild rice. Even though the residents of the North Country hunted wildlife, they respected their surroundings and sought to use its resources responsibly. Hunters took pride in their shooting abilities. A hunter with good aim would take a head shot, leaving the body meat unharmed (and not wasted). A grouse, duck or goose with lead shot in its body was something to be ashamed of, as the meat would go uneaten.

Poor Man's Lobster

The lake itself offered a plethora of delicacies depending on the time of year. During the summer, walleyes were deep-fried, in the fall, whitefish netting helped fill the smoker, and in the winter a lunker northern pike could be used to make what the Finns called *Kala Mojakka*, or fish chowder. A boiled lake trout was perhaps best of all. When served with drawn butter it was known as "poor man's lobster," a meal comparable to any fancy restaurant in the city.

TOP: Five young mallards

BOTTOM: Dorothy and two large northern pike

The Florence Nightingale of the North Woods

Dorothy didn't just have to contend with the weather or a daunting list of chores; as she was one of the only people with medical training nearby, she was the only source of medical help for many people in the area. This became painfully clear in the winter of 1940, when a kidney infection nearly took Bill's life.

When Bill fell ill, Dorothy recognized the severity of the situation. Despite a raging blizzard outside, she packed Bill into a toboggan and started to pull the critically ill man to town. As she had difficulty keeping track of the trail due to the driving snow, the duo was moving much slower than needed. As they arrived at Ensign Lake the darkness prevented them from traveling any further. Fortunately Dorothy knew of an old trapper cabin nearby. It was in a state of disrepair, but it had an old barrel stove that was still in working order; this provided them with enough shelter and warmth for the night. In the early light of dawn, Dorothy was up and moving, as Bill's condition had worsened over the night. Seven hours later they finally arrived at a lodge on Moose Lake, and Dorothy used an old crank phone to call for help. Within the hour a sheriff arrived and Bill was taken to the hospital in Ely. Thanks to Dorothy's nursing ability and strength, Bill was able to enjoy eight more years on the islands he loved so dearly.

ABOVE: Winter weather

Bill's Health Begins to Fail

Even though he recovered from his kidney infection, that daunting episode proved to be the beginning of the end for Bill. Bill's habits of smoking and drinking proved detrimental to this tall, lanky man of the woods, and his health continued to decline as heart disease and the damage of unmanaged diabetes took their toll. Thereafter the heavy chores of running a wilderness fishing camp fell increasingly onto Dorothy's shoulders, a young city girl who had transformed herself to become a woodswoman of the north. As Bill's condition worsened, the relationship between Bill and Dorothy transitioned. Prior to his illness, Bill had been Dorothy's employer, but the relationship quickly became one between a patient and a nurse.

On March 22, 1948, Bill passed away at the hospital in Virginia, Minnesota. He'd suffered a long series of illnesses; he was seventy-three years old. Due to his declining health, Bill's death was somewhat expected, but it was still difficult for Dorothy to lose her longtime friend. As if Bill's death weren't enough, Dorothy was in for a nasty surprise—Bill had always told Dorothy that when he died the islands would be left to her, but Bill had failed to leave a will!

ABOVE: Bill's death certificate

Dorothy (Finally) Comes to Own the Resort

Apparently living fifteen miles and five portages from the nearest road made the idea of going to town to create a will unappealing, and for Bill it was certainly not a priority. Dorothy was devastated and never quite totally forgave Bill for this grievous oversight. Because of this legal limbo, the property went into probate and was eventually given to Bill's brother August Berglund of St. Hilaire, Minnesota, and his sister, Mrs. Kate Johnson of Vashon Island, Washington. Knowing Bill's wishes, August and Kate generously deeded the resort to Dorothy in a simple ceremony at the Lake County Courthouse. No money was exchanged, although the islands were certainly quite valuable at the time. With this simple transaction Dorothy Molter became the sole proprietor of the Isle of Pines resort and remained so for her entire life. As she'd soon find out, property ownership wasn't without its problems.

ABOVE: An aerial view of the Isle of Pines

TOP: Winter at the resort

BOTTOM: A Forest Service memo regarding acquisition of the Isle of Pines

Superior N.F.   Duluth 1, Minn.

Office Memorandum · UNITED STATES GOVERNMENT

FOREST SERVICE
ELY, MINN.
JAN 2 1
RECEIVED

TO   :   Kawishiwi

FROM :   GALEN W. PIKE, Forest Supervisor   DATE: January 20, 1948

SUBJECT: L ACQUISITION, Superior, Purchase, Roadless Area (I.W.L. Berglund)

According to our records, Mr. William J. Berglund, Box 35, Winton, Minnesota, is the owner of Lot 5, Section 31, Township 65 North, Range 7 West (an island in Knife Lake).

We have not been particularly concerned about acquiring this tract for self-evident reasons, but the situation may now be altered. We have recently been informed, by what we believe to be a reliable source, that Mr. Berglund is ill and may require hospitalization. We have no other information on the matter but since Mr. Berglund is along in years, we are wondering if it would not be a good time to try and sew up this tract. If necessary, we should probably take it, even if we have to give Berglund a life estate, since probably such occupancy will not be excessive.

Will you, therefore, contact Mr. Berglund at your convenience and secure his reactions to selling the property? If you are able to make a deal on some reasonable basis, please furnish us with information as to improvements, exact name and address, details of the transaction, etc. and we will draw up the necessary papers for signing.

A reply at your convenience will be appreciated.

Unable to contact since he is very sick in Virginia Hospital

A CHANGING REGION

LETTERS FROM THE GOVERNMENT

Almost immediately after she took ownership of the resort, Dorothy began receiving letters from the government requesting that she sell the property, so it could become part of a large tract of wilderness. In fact, the first letter from the U.S. Forest Service had actually arrived when Bill Berglund still owned the resort but was gravely ill. The audacity of the letter dated January 20, 1948, surely set the tone for the battle that was about to ensue, as it was the first letter in a long series of correspondence. As communication at that time was limited to mail, telegraph or word-of-mouth, it's no surprise that the oft-requested transaction was delayed time and time again. To understand the conflict that Dorothy had inadvertently waded into, a little history is helpful. When Dorothy first visited Knife Lake there was no such thing as the BWCA and the Wilderness Act was still 34 years in the future. Even when she became the owner of the resort, the creation of the BWCA wouldn't occur for another decade, but a number of changes had already occurred that had an impact upon Dorothy and the resort.

The Beginnings of the BWCA

In 1902 the U.S. Land Office withdrew 500,000 acres of land from settlement with the State of Minnesota; this prevented any new settlements from being established there. This land would eventually become part of the BWCA, and other tracts were soon to follow. Further expansion of the area occurred in 1904, after Congress sent a request to the State Forestry Board for 20,000 acres to be set aside; this led to the creation of the Burntside Forest Reserve. The area expanded again from 1905–1908, when General C.C. Andrews persuaded the U.S. Land Office to withdraw an additional 659,700 acres from the state settlement increasing the area to over 1,150,000 acres. As the name indicates, forest reserves were dedicated to help produce timber for the logging industry. This wasn't their only use, however. According to the Minnesota Forestry Commissioners Report of 1905, the "State Forest Reserves should be devoted not alone to the business of raising timber, but to the pleasure of all the people." The forest reserves weren't created just to raise timber—importantly, they were also established to provide residents with a wide range of recreational opportunities. This correlation would prove quite important, as a large swath of essentially untouched land was dedicated (at least partially) to recreation. This would help lay the groundwork for many of the arguments in favor of the creation of the BWCA.

In 1909, President Theodore Roosevelt created the Superior National Forest (SNF) from previously withdrawn domain lands after observing the decline of game animals while on expeditions throughout the U.S. While Roosevelt was famous as a hunter and naturalist, he was also a forceful voice for conservation. In the September 1913 issue of *Scribner's Magazine*, he wrote, "Far more interesting than the chase itself is the observation, the study of the life histories of the strange and wonderful creatures of the wilderness." In that year the Minnesota Legislature created the 1,200,000-acre Superior Game Refuge, which was similar in size to the Superior National Forest, and included most of the present-day BWCA. The game refuge was created in an attempt to save threatened moose and caribou populations; hunting restrictions were also put into effect.

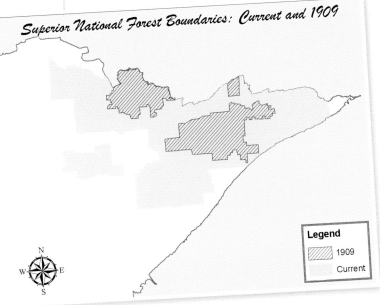

ABOVE: The boundaries of the Superior National Forest over time

Roads Into the Wilderness

Between 1922 and 1926 three roads—the Echo Trail, the Upper Gunflint Trail, and Fernberg Road—were developed in the previously roadless Superior National Forest to help make the wilderness more accessible for recreation. The Fernberg Road, which heads east out of Ely, provided Dorothy with access to Moose Lake, the first lake on her journey to the Isle of Pines. In order to prevent the area from being overrun with roads, U.S. Agriculture Secretary W. M. Jardine designated 640,000 acres within the Superior National Forest as roadless wilderness. This policy was enacted to "retain as much as possible of the land which has recreational opportunities of this nature as a wilderness." This designation made it clear that wilderness was inherently valuable for recreation. Even though the creation of the BWCA wouldn't occur for over three decades, this distinction would continue to become more prominent and important.

The next major piece of congressional legislation pertaining to the future BWCA was the Shipstead-Newton-Nolan Act, which passed in 1930. A group of wealthy power investors had intended to install a series of eighty-foot-high electricity-generating dams along the borders; thankfully, pressure from an international coalition of conservation and environmental groups resulted in the passage of the Shipstead-Newton-Nolan Act, which prevented the construction of the dams. If the dam system had been put in place the lakes region would undoubtedly have been destroyed. It would be the Thye-Blatnik Act of 1948, however, that would have the longest-lasting impact on Dorothy's life on the Isle of Pines.

ABOVE: Dorothy pointing out the Isle of Pines on a border country map

What Is A Wilderness?

By 1948, the debate about what constituted a wilderness—and what activities and equipment should permitted in the wilderness—began to dominate much of public life in the region. Preservation groups such as the Izaak Walton League felt that the wilderness should be limited to canoe-campers and they argued that motorboats and large commercial resort operations should be banned from the wilderness. This ruffled some feathers because Ely was known as "The Playground of the Nation." On Basswood Lake alone, there were twenty resorts, which catered primarily to the wealthy patrons of the era. The Thye-Blatnik Act authorized and directed the U.S. Forest Service to acquire lands within an area covering about two-thirds of the present-day Boundary Waters Canoe Area. It carried an authorization of $500,000, creating a fund to buy out private property owners. U.S. Forest Service employees soon began contacting property owners in an attempt to arrange purchase of tracts of land, including Dorothy's. Nevertheless, it wasn't the local faction of USFS employees that deemed her presence a detriment to the area; instead, there was a push on the federal level to return some natural areas to their previous state of wilderness.

Dorothy's Angels

As more legislation was passed, wilderness travel became more difficult. This increasingly became a quandary for Dorothy. It would be a faction of locals nicknamed "Dorothy's Angels" that would eventually help Dorothy cope with all the changes. Some of the first "angels" were the pilots Bill Leithol, Chick Beel and Hoot Hautala, who brought in gear and supplies for Dorothy. Some trips she paid for and others the pilots completed through the goodness of their heart or in exchange for a good, strong cup of black coffee.

TOP: Floatplanes were used to fly-in wooden cases of glass bottles of soda

BOTTOM: Dorothy stands on the float of a plane

...ane Ban

...lights didn't last, however. In 1949, right on the heels of the
... President Truman issued an executive order prohibiting
...g on lakes and flights below 4,000 feet. Preservation
...e parties arriving in floatplanes were overfishing the
...tinued flights would open the area up for the potential of
...nent. This decision would eventually prove problematic for
...ly didn't affect her until 1952. Up until that point, rogue
...ing into the wilderness and delivering supplies as a way of
...sion. It wasn't until a local pilot's plane was confiscated and
...gal flights that these renegade trips ended.

...planes meant that it was nearly impossible to haul large
...upplies for the upcoming summer season. Only essential
...ed to run the resort were hauled over the five portages.
... in wooden crates were certainly not vital to the
...was undeterred by these decisions; on the contrary,
...-on and adjusted to accommodate each fresh
...city would serve her well in the years to come, as
...ntroversial piece of legislation would restrict travel

> Friends are the
> flowers in the
> garden of life.

TOP: The rugged portage trails made traveling (and transporting supplies) a bit of a challenge for Dorothy

BOTTOM: A typical portage in the BWCA

Trips in the Summer

A guest's journey to the Isle of Pines took some planning and coordination. The days when the wealthy could hire a pilot and plane and be fishing within an hour were gone. Instead, the only option was to portage and canoe. The word portage is French for "to carry" and portaging refers to carrying a watercraft over an established trail that links two bodies of water. This made it difficult to reach Knife Lake and Dorothy's resort, as it was fifteen miles (and five portages) away from the nearest road at Moose Lake. A journey to the resort went like this: Launching from the landing at Moose Lake, a motorboat would tow the canoe for seven miles through Newfound and Sucker Lakes. After this, one would arrive at the northeast end of Birch Lake, where the first portage would be crossed. Once across the first portage, gear and passengers were loaded into a large square-sterned aluminum canoe outfitted with a small outboard motor. The next three portages were quite short, and covered the terrain through Carp, Melon and Seed Lakes. The final portage, sometimes referred to as "Big Knife," was a quarter-mile long. Once travelers finally crossed that last portage, they could see Robbin's Island in the distance, as well as their ultimate destination, the Isle of Pines Resort. Thankfully, if the water levels were high enough, all of the portages except one could possibly be avoided by simply wading up the mild rapids located near the portages. This meant the traveling party wouldn't have to unload their gear, carry it over the portage, and reload it. This saved time and a tremendous amount of backbreaking labor.

ABOVE: Dorothy using a boat and a canoe to help visitors reach Knife Lake

Skis and Sled Dogs in the Winter

Winter travel was just as difficult. Prior to the use of snowmobiles, there were three ways to travel to Knife Lake in the winter—on skis, snowshoes, or by sled dog teams. During the coldest parts of the year a more direct route was possible through Splash Lake, Ensign Lake, and over a frozen swamp that connected to Vera Lake. This shaved off about three miles from the traveling distance compared to the summer boating route.

More Join the Ranks of Dorothy's Angels

With the additional travel restrictions, Dorothy needed more help. Thankfully, others were there to help her; Dorothy's Angels didn't just consist of helpful floatplane pilots. For many years Dorothy was helped out by various friends who owned businesses on or near Moose Lake or lived in the area; these folks included Hollis Latourell, Laurel Bennett, Bernie Carlson, Emery Bulinski and Bob Cary, among others. If they happened to be going to Knife Lake themselves or sending an employee up to the lake in a motorboat they would bring anything Dorothy needed or supplies she had left stored at Moose Lake. Many local fishing guides like Norm Saari and Mike Patterson helped too; they brought in supplies, carried out mail, or sent messages back to town.

Larry and Myrt Sernak of Aurora, Minnesota, are good examples of how Dorothy's Angels went out of their way to help her. While reminiscing Larry said, "I worked for the railroad and in the winter I was laid off. Myrt and I would run up there and caretake the cabins so Dorothy could go visit her family in Chicago without worrying about her property. Knife Lake sure had good fishing and that water made the best Jello! Myrt and Dorothy just loved to play that damn Scramble [Scrabble]. They would sit down at the kitchen table in the Winter Cabin and not say a word to each other for hours. Finally I put an end to it because they would stay up so late that Myrt wouldn't want to get up and go fishing the next morning!"

ABOVE: Dorothy and Myrt Sernak play a game of Scrabble while friend Pete Spehar looks on

The End of Soda Pop, but the Beginning of Root Beer

Even with the help, the travel restrictions made it impossible to bring in the dozens of wooden cases filled with glass bottles of soda pop. In the documentary *Living in the Boundary Waters*, she says, "I used to have pop, but after the planes quite flying, well then I discontinued it because I wasn't about to pack pop over the portages. There's too much of it, and I don't think anybody else would care for the job, either." As Dorothy said in the documentary, "I had so many root beer bottles on hand, I kept them for a few years and finally I was cleaning one day, and I ran across those bottles and I was wondering what to do with them. So then we got the idea of making root beer." In a strange way, the travel restrictions indirectly led her to become the root beer lady.

Dorothy's new root beer didn't lack customers. The wild expanse that would become the BWCA became increasingly popular with tourists. For paddlers who had been drinking tepid lake water for days on end, the prospect of enjoying an ice-cold root beer was alluring, and the idea caught on fast. In the heat of the summer Dorothy often had 150–200 visitors a day. Soon Dorothy would be brewing and selling between eleven and twelve thousand bottles of her home brew a summer. Occasionally the demand for root beer became so great that she put out a sign that read, "Limit: Two root beers." On one occasion when Dorothy ran out of extract, the sign was painted over, and visitors were limited to just one root beer.

TOP: Dorothy standing outside the Summer Tent
MIDDLE: Dorothy ladling a fresh brew of root beer
BOTTOM: Dorothy taking on a familiar task—bottling

Visits from Family

Despite the travel restrictions and the many visitors she received, Dorothy often found time to entertain family. After tragically losing their mother when they were young, the Molter siblings developed quite a strong bond with one another. In particular, Dorothy's sister Ruth (one year older) and her brother William "Bud" Molter (three years younger) spent a good amount of time at the resort helping out during the summers.

Bud Molter

Dorothy's brother Bud was a jovial man and the instigator of all the quirky signs and structures that were scattered about on the Summer Tent island; these provided entertainment to guests and passing canoeists alike. One example of Bud's handiwork was an old broken paddle stenciled with the phrase "Even a fish can avoid trouble if he keeps his mouth shut"; this was nailed onto a tree directly below the famous "KWITCHURBELIAKIN" sign. Bud also created a wood cutout of a police officer holding his hand up, and this was placed next to a parking meter that was cemented into the shoreline near the boat landing. The sign on the parking meter stated, "Please do not use coins. This meter has been converted to accept dollar bills only." Among Bud's other engineering feats, he created a throne constructed of beer cans and a small replica airplane with a propeller fashioned out of broken paddle blades. Perhaps Bud's most famous work was a hand-painted sign that read, "-WE DON'T MAKE MISTEAKS-ANY IMPERFECKSHUN IS AN INJINEARING MISCALCULASHUN EVEN A JENEOUS CAIN'T ALWAYS BE PURRFECT."

TOP: Evidence of Bud's antics

MIDDLE: The police officer halts canoe traffic

BOTTOM: KWITCHURBELIAKIN, one of the funniest signs on the island, and a phrase still popular today

Ruth (Molter) Crozier

Just a year older than Dorothy, Ruth (Molter) Crozier shared her sister's spirit and love of the North Woods. She also provided Dorothy with a dose of female companionship that her life was probably lacking at times. Ruth originally stayed for short visits in the summer, but she began to spend full summers on the island in the mid-1970s after she was widowed and retired from her job. Together Dorothy and Ruth made beaded Christmas ornaments and dolls out of pinecones, and played card and board games late into the night.

Staking Out a Bear

Another of Dorothy's sisters, Helen, also visited Knife Lake, and she was involved in one particularly memorable incident—a stakeout of a bear. According to Dorothy's Christmas letters, one particular late night involved a two-hour stakeout as Dorothy and Helen waited for a nuisance bear to return to the scene of its crime. Earlier that evening, just as everyone had turned in for the night, a couple staying in the Point Cabin came running quickly to the Summer Tent and reported that a bear had crashed through a screen door on the porch, toppling the icebox. As the guests chased it away by making a ruckus with banging of pots and pans, the bear absconded with one of their bags of clothing. Rifle in hand, Dorothy and Helen posted themselves outside that cabin, but the effort was all for naught, as the bear didn't return. Walking back to the tent in the dark Dorothy saw something shiny and white in the beam of her flashlight. It turned out to be a very delicate pair of women's panties that most likely had fallen out of the clothing bag as the bear had lumbered off. Holding the panties up to her portly midriff she shook her head and whispered to her dear sister, "Looks like that bear scared the lady right out of her pants."

TOP LEFT: Ruth shows off a large lake trout

TOP RIGHT: Ruth and Dorothy on the steps of the Winter Cabin

BOTTOM: Dorothy and Ruth enjoy a cup of coffee in the Summer Tent

Furry (and Feathery) Friends

While Dorothy may have chased a bear or two off in her time, she was also quite a friend to the animals of the area. On occasion, she even served as a nurse for animals. In particular, Dorothy helped two minks, which she named Mickey and Stinky. Mickey was found in a trap with a broken leg and Stinky was tiny and only about two weeks old when it entered Dorothy's care. They both grew up to be strong adults.

Dorothy helped birds too. A crow named Vera Tick was one of Dorothy's most notable avian patients. Dorothy found the bird on the Vera Lake Portage during prime tick season (hence its name); too young to fly, Vera Tick broke a wing after falling from a tree. Dorothy fed the bird by hand using a medicine dropper, and Vera grew to be a loud, squawking resident of the island with a penchant for pilfering small objects, such as bottle caps, nails or even clothespins. Vera's most famous heist occurred when she stole dentures from Dorothy's sister Ruth. Ruth had quite a fight with Vera while wrestling to get her teeth back, something Dorothy later wished she had on film.

TOP: An adult black bear

MIDDLE: Black bear cubs

BOTTOM: Dorothy and Vera Tick, the crow Dorothy nursed back to health

Cap, Dorothy's Father, Becomes a Regular

In 1940, Dorothy had been working permanently at the resort for over six years when her father Cap, stepmother Myrtle, and sister Ruth came to stay for a long visit. During that vacation, which lasted from July 14th to September 21st, John "Cap" Molter's vacation journal relates that he spent forty-seven of those days fishing. To say he was an angling fanatic is an understatement.

Retirement and the loss of his second wife prompted Cap to become a seasonal resident of the resort. He usually arrived in March before the ice-out and headed back home to Chicago sometime in October before freeze-up. Instantly recognizable with his captain's hat, buffalo-plaid jacket, and pipe, Cap became a Knife Lake institution. Cap's fierce commitment to his family as a young widower had made a lasting and indelible bond between father and daughter. Dorothy was glad to have his company, not to mention his help with chores, such as putting up firewood or serving as a fishing guide for customers who weren't having too much luck catching fish on their own.

Cap had another reason to visit Knife Lake in the 1950s, after pressure from resort owners and sport fishermen prompted the state to stock smallmouth bass in the border lakes. The smallmouth bass offered a fishing experience unlike any other, as its fighting ability and acrobatic jumps endeared it to anglers throughout the region. The species adapted well to the fishery, creating another draw to the area for anticipatory anglers. Capitalizing on this added good fortune, Cap rarely missed a day of going out on the water and was happy to share his excess catch with visitors for them to enjoy or take home.

TOP: Cap with his characteristic pipe

BOTTOM: Cap and Dorothy

The Invention of the Snowmobile

With the invention of the snowmobile in the 1950s, travel to the resort became easier in the winter, and members of the area snowmobile clubs began to help Dorothy out. Established in 1960, the Ely Igloos Snowmobile Club was the first of its kind, and with increasingly reliable snowmachines it was easy to haul supplies over the frozen lakes in a more direct route to the islands. John and Peg Rosett were active members of the club and made frequent trips up to Dorothy's.

As Peg explained, "Usually one weekend of the winter would be a Dorothy Molter day. We would load up whatever items Dorothy needed and bring them up there by snowmobile. I had the lightest load so I would get up there first. Can you guess what it was? Toilet paper! A light load, but an important one! When we arrived she would have the old barrel stove out on the lake with a big pot of soup on it. It was just the best soup, a meal in itself. She would have a honey-do list for the guys and one way or another, the things she needed help with would get done."

The snowmobile didn't just provide Dorothy with another way to transport goods; it also made traveling to the resort in the winter possible for Cap. As Cap was then in his seventies and struggled with weak legs that were damaged by diabetes, attempting to walk or snowshoe the twelve-mile winter route from Knife Lake to Moose Lake would have been impossible. They had some harrowing adventures with those early machines, but thanks to snowmobiles, Dorothy was fortunate enough to be able to spend more time with her father.

TOP: Wind sleds were used in the '50s; powered by airplane props, they weighed 500 lbs and traveled between 30 and 70 mph, depending on snow conditions

MIDDLE: Dorothy on a snowmobile

BOTTOM: Cap on the 1957 Polaris Snow Traveler

Cap Dies . . .

Cap's thirty-one years of sojourns to his beloved Isle of Pines came
to an end on May 7th of 1962, just one day after Dorothy's fifty-
fifth birthday. In Bob Cary's *Root Beer Lady*, Dorothy recalled, "May
seventh, Cap got up as usual. He went down to the dock, getting ready
to go fishin'. The trout had been hitting and he had been out the day
before with some luck. But after a few minutes he came back to the
tent to lay down. Suddenly, he said he couldn't get his breath, and
before anything could be done, he passed away." As it turned out,
Dorothy was to have little respite from sorrow. Just at the sharpness
of her loss began to dull, another heartache took its place.

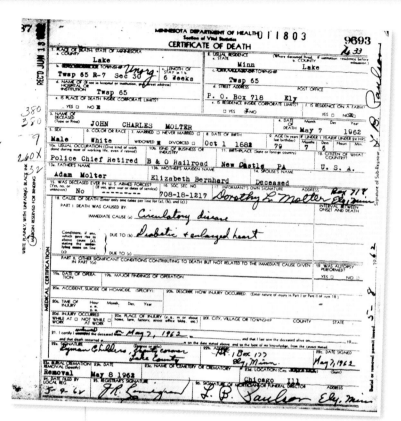

ABOVE: Cap's death certificate

ABOVE: Cap on the beer can throne

ABOVE: The icehouse in winter
RIGHT: A 1952 letter from the Forest Service

WARNING
YOU MUST HAVE YOUR
FISHING LICENSE ON YOUR
PERSON WHEN FISHING
DEPARTMENT OF CONSERVATION
DIVISION OF GAME AND

February 18, 1952

L
ACQUISITION, Superior
Purchase
Roadless Area
Molter, Dorothy L.
(Knife Lake)

Miss Dorothy L. Molter
Box 725
Ely, Minnesota

Dear Miss Molter:

From time to time for several years we have discussed with you
the possibility of the government acquiring your property on Knife
Lake described as Lot 5, Section 31, T 65 N, R 7 W.

We are still interested in acquiring the property and will be
pleased at any time to give immediate, serious consideration to
any proposal you may wish to make.

Very truly yours,

GALEN W. PIKE
Forest Supervisor

By WAYNE SWORD, Acting

cc - Kawishiwi

FOREST SERVICE
ELY MINN
FEB 19
RECEIVED

TROUBLE WITH THE GOVERNMENT

APPRAISALS AND OFFERS

As a resort owner, Dorothy was painfully aware of the burden the travel restrictions put upon her. But as the old adage goes, "necessity is the mother of invention," and Dorothy managed to survive—and even prosper—despite the challenges. Over the years Dorothy received letters from the Forest Service requesting that she sell her property. While the letters listed appraised values and monetary offerings, each time Dorothy refused to sell. She felt their appraisals were far below what the islands were worth, both monetarily and sentimentally. In 1958, the controversy continued to simmer. That year, the Superior Roadless Area was renamed the Boundary Waters Canoe Area (BWCA). The public soon became intensely interested in the issue, and debates about logging, access roads, and the use of motors and snowmobiles soon became contentious and began to dominate public life. Arguments about these issues filled the editorial pages of local newspapers.

More Letters from the Forest Service

Despite the travel restrictions, Dorothy was determined to stay, so you can imagine her amusement from the letter of July 14, 1960. A form was enclosed with the letter, and all she had to do was fill it out, sign it, and return it, as if the Forest Service expected her to have a change of heart on a whim and agree to sell. As the years had passed, she'd received many letters, but their tone had begun to change as well. Instead of requests to buy the property, the letters began to sound more like demands.

The controversy rose to the forefront in 1964 when U.S. Agriculture Secretary Orville Freeman appointed the Selke Committee to recommend changes to management of the wilderness area. This committee was tasked with creating a legal definition of wilderness; the eventual definition they produced is " . . . an area where the earth and its community of life are untrammeled by man, where man himself is a visitor who does not remain." Following the Selke Committee's recommendations, Congress passed the Wilderness Act and President Lyndon B. Johnson signed it into law. Dorothy soon realized that this definition of wilderness meant that she could no longer remain on the Isle of Pines.

5420

FOREST SERVICE
JUL 15 1960

July 14, 1960

Miss Dorothy L. Molter
Box 725
Ely, Minnesota

Dear Miss Molter:

As you undoubtedly know, the Forest Service has been directed to purchase the private lands within the Boundary Waters Canoe Area. Money for this purpose was included in this year's appropriation bill, and we are accordingly contacting owners, preparing appraisals, etc.

We would like very much to receive an offer from you, and you may use for this purpose one copy of the enclosed offer form, which should be filled out as completely as possible.

Should you desire to discuss the situation either before or after completing the form, please advise and we will be pleased to meet with you at your convenience.

Your assistance is appreciated.

Yours very truly,

L. P. Neff, Forest Supervisor

By L. A. Anselment, Acting

Enclosures

cc:
cc: Kawishiwi

pc 7/29

ABOVE: The July 14th, 1960, letter from the USFS

Forced to Move?

When the Wilderness Act of 1964 designated the BWCA as a unit of the National Wilderness Preservation System, the USFS became legally authorized to employ the right of eminent domain on tracts that had not otherwise been acquired. This meant that the government had the legal right to take the land, as long as that acquisition was for the public good. For Dorothy, it looked like it was the beginning of the end for her time on the Isle of Pines. In a final letter from April 23, 1964, the Forest Service declared that condemnation of her property was the only option available.

As the debates raged about what activities should be allowed in the wilderness, Dorothy worried. First, the public dispute was disconcerting for Dorothy. She worried about not knowing how she would get supplies in, and wondered angrily how the locals, some no longer young or strong, would fare making the daunting journey to their favorite fishing hole or campsite.

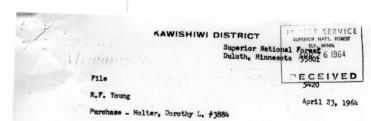

ABOVE: The final letter from the USFS

Benny Ambrose:
A Neighbor in a Similar Situation

As it happened, Dorothy wasn't the only person in danger of losing land due to passage of the Wilderness Act. Her story wouldn't be complete without an introduction to her closest neighbor, Benny Ambrose, who lived ten miles to the northeast. Benny was a pioneer of the wilderness on Ottertrack Lake, and the second-to-last legal resident of the Boundary Waters Canoe Area Wilderness. After being discharged from the U.S. Army in 1919, he was lured to the great North Woods of Minnesota. Benny had served in the Army with an Ojibwe man who told him about the border lakes region and possible precious metals, including gold. He didn't find gold, but he found that living in the area was a treasure in itself.

When one first approached Benny's cabin, his talent for gardening was obvious. He had mastered the art of farming while living and working on southern Minnesota farms. When he moved up north for good, he brought that dirt along with him to use in his garden; he hauled canoe loads of it over portages to his hilltop home on Ottertrack Lake. He put that soil to use well; he excelled at growing an ample supply of food. Dorothy was a frequent recipient of Benny's produce in late summer. Dorothy was especially fond of his fresh, ripe tomatoes.

TOP: Benny Ambrose's cabin on Ottertrack Lake

BOTTOM: Benny's garden plot

By all accounts, Benny was content on his land, as he'd been there for decades. When local Forest Service employees visited his cabin and talk of possible condemnation was in the air, Benny allegedly gestured to a high-powered rifle and said, "The next government employee to come knocking at my door won't be returning."

A Friend in Need . . .

Dorothy Molter had a good friend in Bob Cary; both of them had grown up in Chicago and they each had a passion for the North Woods of Minnesota. They'd known each other for years, and as a former staff writer for the outdoors section of the *Chicago Daily News*, Bob knew of a way to help his dear old friend. He wrote a news story that described the Root Beer Lady's precarious situation. The story was picked up nationally and there was a huge groundswell of support for Dorothy.

ABOVE: Benny Ambrose in his kitchen

A Friend to Many

Many people in the region knew of Dorothy because of her root beer, but just as many knew her for her kindness, generosity and willingness to help others. During the course of her years on the Isle of Pines she had served others with a rare selflessness, all the while never expecting favors in return for her kind deeds. It was this character trait that served her well when her time of need became apparent.

Despite her geographical isolation, Dorothy had gradually become one of the most celebrated and well-known residents of the North Woods, yet she wasn't known nationally until the early 1950s. The earliest indication of Dorothy's growing celebrity came in the form of a cartoon drawn by journalist Glen Sternkopf. His dagwoodesque cartoon depicts a group visiting the BWCA; instead of as people, the canoeists are portrayed as pack horses loaded with gear. Sternkopf had visited Dorothy and the BWCA with a group that included Bill Shrout, photographer for *The Saturday Evening Post*, and Andrew Hamilton, a freelance writer and the public affairs officer at the University of California, Los Angeles. After this trip, Hamilton wrote an article for *The Saturday Evening Post* entitled, "The Loneliest Woman in America," which was published in October of 1952.

ABOVE: Glen Sternkopf's cartoon

LEFT: Dorothy and *The Saturday Evening Post* cover

A Media Spectacle

Given the frequent visits by friends, family and passing canoeists, Dorothy was hardly lonely, even though she lived amid the wilderness, so the *Post* title was misleading, to say the least. Nevertheless, despite the title, the *Saturday Evening Post* article introduced Dorothy and her plight to the nation. Soon more and more reporters, journalists, and even television crews were drawn to the BWCA. In the ensuing years, Dorothy was the subject of dozens of articles, including pieces by all sorts of publications, from small midwestern publications to major newspapers like the *Minneapolis Star and Tribune*, the *St. Paul Pioneer Press*, and the *Chicago Tribune*. Even sensationalist magazines like *The National Enquirer* and *The National Tattler* joined in and voiced their opinions about her dilemma with the government.

While Dorothy was already popular locally, when she became nationally known she received more and more attention from the regional media. In particular, she was featured in short news segments on local television stations in Duluth and Minneapolis, further increasing her fan base. These television clips, filmed amid the beautiful setting of the Isle of Pines, were particularly important, as they gave viewers a glimpse of her world. Television also did something that print couldn't do—it captured Dorothy's gentle voice and laid-back demeanor, introducing viewers to the person that so many people had found endearing. This, in turn, brought more visitors to Knife Lake in the summer.

ABOVE: Dorothy with visitors, including a reporter from *Time Magazine*

More Than Just Root Beer

Much of the attention that Dorothy received was due to her famous root beer, but she was nearly as famous for the medical care that she provided to those in need in the wilderness. A registered nurse, Dorothy was deftly able to remove embedded fishhooks, bandage up gashes, and provide first aid when serious accidents occurred. It's no surprise that area outfitters put a star next to her island on the map when routing guests through the wilderness. "If you run into a problem," they'd say, "you can always go to Dorothy's for help."

Whether they visited Dorothy for her root beer, for medical care, or just to meet the woman they'd heard so much about, visitors flocked to the Isle of Pines. Starting in 1955, Dorothy kept track of how many visitors she received each day in simple spiral-bound notebooks. She averaged between six and seven thousand visitors per season to her wilderness home. July was the busiest month; she frequently had successive days with more than one hundred visitors. During those times campers were asked to limit their visits to twenty minutes. Dorothy would comment that she would have to "practically take a bath in the middle of the night to have any privacy." People often wondered how Dorothy dealt with all this attention; she freely admitted that the sudden interest in her personal life could be grating, but more often than not she was delighted to be a part of the spotlight.

TOP: Dorothy welcoming guests

BOTTOM: Dorothy poses with visitors

Friends in High Places

All of this attention couldn't have come at a better time, as Dorothy's land faced condemnation, and the prospects of remaining at the Isle of Pines were looking bleak. Thankfully, there was a tremendous public outcry of support for Dorothy, and the Forest Service was besieged with letters and phone calls. The Forest Service also received a number of petitions in support of Dorothy, and these featured thousands of signatures. Dorothy even had the support of Minnesota Senator Hubert Humphrey, who would soon become the Vice President in the Johnson administration. Whatever their connection, people came out in droves to support Dorothy; in the end, her kindnesses were returned tenfold, and this collaborative effort is what allowed her to stay on her beloved Isle of Pines.

The USFS and Dorothy Make a Deal

With so much public pressure, the Forest Service negotiated with Dorothy. She agreed to sell her property to the U.S. government for $39,000 with the stipulation that, for a fee of $14,210, she could remain on her property until 1975. In total, she received $24,790 for her land. The USFS probably assumed that since Dorothy would be 68 in 1975, she'd be ready to retire and move to an easier life in Ely. Nevertheless, as the years went by, Dorothy was still going strong and showed no signs of slowing down, and had no intention of moving to town.

TOP: Hubert Humphrey

BOTTOM: An outside view of Dorothy's Summer Tent, with her brother Bud's silly signs; she sold her root beer right out of an old Coca Cola cooler with a block of lake ice to keep it cold

Lifetime Tenancy

The Forest Service knew that if they evicted Dorothy in 1975, they'd have another fight on their hands, one that would result in more negative publicity. To avoid this, the Forest Service drafted a plan to make Dorothy and Benny Ambrose U.S. Forest Service volunteers-in-service in exchange for lifetime tenancy. According to the agreement, Benny and Dorothy would be permitted to live on their land for the rest of their lives. After they passed away, their land would be incorporated into the wilderness and no additional full-time residents would be permitted in the BWCA.

Their agreement with the Superior National Forest Supervisor came with several conditions. In particular, Dorothy was asked to:

1. Keep records of the number of people visiting Knife Lake, summer and winter.

2. Assist and provide information to BWCA visitors in the Knife Lake area.

3. Monitor campsite occupancy on the western end of Knife Lake to determine frequency of overnight use for establishing user travel patterns.

All of these tasks would help the Forest Service plan how to manage the area more effectively in the future.

ABOVE: A campsite in the present-day BWCA

Easier Said Than Done

Both Dorothy and Benny agreed with this proposal, but implementing it wasn't easy. The Wilderness Act was already federal law, and to change a federal law, it must first be amended in a bill, which must then be passed by both houses of Congress and signed by the President to take effect. Thankfully, in 1972 Congressman Andrew Jacobs, Jr of the Eleventh Congressional District of Indiana introduced a bill, House Resolution 17168, allowing Dorothy and Benny to remain lifetime residents of the BWCA. The bill, which was entitled "For the Relief of Dorothy Molter," was aptly named, and after 25 years of fighting to remain on her cherished islands, Dorothy was undoubtedly very relieved. Dorothy was finally free to remain on her land.

While Dorothy had been at odds with the Forest Service for much of her life, once the status of her residency was settled, employees for the USFS became Dorothy's Angels as well. Such members of the Forest Service staff paddled through the wilderness, checked canoeists for permits, and cleaned up campsites and portage trails. They'd often check in on Dorothy and became fond of her. In addition, USFS floatplanes brought in Dorothy's family members and large loads of equipment, such as tanks of propane, gasoline or root beer-making supplies. Sunflowers seeds and corn were flown in by the ton to keep the island ducks happy and the bird feeders filled.

92D CONGRESS
2D SESSION

H. R. 17168

IN THE HOUSE OF REPRESENTATIVES

OCTOBER 13, 1972

Mr. JACOBS introduced the following bill; which was referred to the Committee on Interior and Insular Affairs

A BILL

For relief of Dorothy Molter.

1   *Be it enacted by the Senate and House of Representa-*
2   *tives of the United States of America in Congress assembled,*
3   That notwithstanding section 5 (a) of the Wilderness Act
4   or any other provision of law, Dorothy Molter shall not be
5   required during her lifetime to exchange for federally-owned
6   land any real property she owns near Knife Lake in the
7   Boundary Waters Canoe Area, Minnesota. Dorothy Molter
8   has provided recognizable service to the users of such area
9   by rendering medical assistance, as a registered nurse, during
10   the thirty-six-year period she has lived near Knife Lake.

III

ABOVE: House Resolution 17168, a Bill for Relief of Dorothy Molter

Other Benefits

Dorothy's special status as a Forest Service volunteer allowed her to keep a boat and motor for use; however, they were only to be used by Dorothy or her immediate family. As Dorothy aged, she needed more help around the islands. Dorothy's Angels helped with the more strenuous chores such as putting up wood and cutting ice, along with many individual staff members from the Charles L. Sommers Boy Scout Base (now known as the Northern Tier High Adventure Base) and the Voyageur Outward Bound School.

ABOVE: Young visitors often interviewed Dorothy about her long life on the Isle of Pines and Knife Lake

ABOVE: Tools hanging on the outside of the icehouse

ABOVE: A young man caps the bottles after Dorothy fills them with root beer

RIGHT: Dorothy stands outside her Trading Post, ready to sell candy and root beer

SOUVENIRS

LIFE AS THE ROOT BEER LADY

BREWING ROOT BEER

The popularity of Dorothy's root beer, when combined with the publicity stemming from her very public dispute with the Forest Service, made her into a celebrity of the North Woods, and droves of canoeists visited Knife Lake each summer. Of course, these visitors wanted to sample Dorothy's famous root beer, and Dorothy often needed assistance keeping up with the demand. Thankfully, Dorothy's friends and family helped her produce it year after year. Dorothy's great-nephew Steve (the son of Dorothy's nephew John and his wife Loretta) is a good example of this. One of the first things Steve learned to do during his apprenticeship and stay at the island was help Auntie Dorothy and Auntie Ruth make root beer. Between 1976 and 1986 Steve helped brew an average of over 10,000 bottles of root beer per summer.

Under the tutelage of his older brother Jay, who was just coming off three summers spent on the island, Steve learned how to complete resort chores. He made trips to town for supplies, fetched guests at the portage, picked up paper garbage and burned it, composted food garbage, and made the evening rounds to the guest cabins, collecting fish guts, filling water containers, and checking the iceboxes. If the boxes needed ice he would head to the icehouse to grab a 2x2 chunk of ice and cut it down to size. The icehouse was one of his favorite places. "It sat peacefully in the big pines and [Uncle] Bud and I would hide Budweiser in there and get ice often. Sometimes it took a while to return." Of course, Steve and his brother Jay made sure to find time for some shenanigans as well.

The Journey of Ribbon Rock

One of the most memorable instances of mischief involved a unique birthday present for Dorothy. On the Canadian shoreline, just a short distance from the resort, there was a large boulder that consisted of a banded iron formation. Its beautiful ribbons of magnetite, jasper and chert made it quite a sight to see. It was unlike the other rocks present in the area, and was probably carried to that location by a glacier about ten thousand years before. Dorothy had always admired the rock, so the boys decided to bring it to her for her birthday.

There was one slight problem. As the boulder consisted largely of magnetite, it was heavy, about three hundred and fifty pounds per cubic foot. The rock was at least four feet square. At a minimum, it weighed twelve hundred pounds. The boys were undeterred. Using a pry bar they lifted the rock up, inch-by-inch, shoving small rocks underneath to create a large crevasse. Then they stood the boat on edge and rolled the rock into the boat with a shove. Steve explained what happened next, "It rolled in beautifully, except it was too far back in the boat and the boat sank!" This meant they had to start over. They managed to move the rock toward the center of the boat, and they positioned two guys in the front of the boat, for counterbalance. After bailing like madmen, they were able to float the boat and began heading for Dorothy's

TOP: A close-up photo of the famous Ribbon Rock presented to Dorothy on her birthday

BOTTOM: Andy Levar observes as the needle of his compass dances around; the magnetite in the rock prevents an accurate reading

camp. Because of all the holes they'd put in the boat, they had to bail water all the way back. They just made it back to the camp, when Dorothy confronted them. Steve still remembers her standing there with her hands on her hips crying out, "What did you do to my boat?!"

Dorothy's Response

Trying to smooth things over, Jay said "Look, Aunt Dorothy, we brought you your favorite rock for your birthday present!"

Dorothy wasn't impressed. "But what did you do to my boat? Why did it just sink?" she asked.

Jay responded, "But look at the nice rock! Where do you want it?"

Realizing the heartfelt intention of their gift, Dorothy forgave them, but got her revenge by making them move and turn the rock a few times until it was placed just so. Fortunately there happened to be a group of tourists around to help them in the process. Chuck Cary, a member of a group of guys that stayed a majority of the summer on Knife Lake was a good friend to Dorothy and helped solder the nine holes that had been put in the boat during the process. The boat never really was the same after that, so Dorothy ended up having to buy a new boat and that old one was reduced to being the wood hauler.

Along with visits from Steve and Jay, Dorothy was visited by many other members of her extended family; helping out Aunt Dorothy was interspersed with swimming, fishing, canoeing and lounging about the island. Great-nephew Danny Galante and his sister Laura each spent time during their teen years helping out Dorothy on the island.

TOP: Dorothy and her sister, Ruth, receive family visitors

BOTTOM: Dorothy and Ruth with more visitors

Benny Ambrose Dies

In August of 1982, Benny Ambrose passed away at the age of 84. Benny was Dorothy's nearest neighbor and the only other permanent resident in the BWCA. He was also a well-known guide, trapper and prospector. His body was discovered near his cabin in August next to the burned-out remains of a canvas shelter where he cooked in the summer. It takes a bit of exploring, but on the United States side of Ottertrack Lake, a stack of native rocks remains a tribute to Dorothy's closest neighbor. Across the border one can also find a plaque that bears his name and the dates he lived; his date of birth is unknown and is marked by a question mark.

ABOVE: Benny's daughters (Holly and Bonnie) scatter his ashes at Ottertrack Lake by canoe

The Last Woman in the Wilderness

After Benny died, Dorothy was the last resident of the BWCA. Thankfully, she had many visitors, but she wasn't just visited by family. Over the years she entertained government bigwigs and prominent anglers alike, but the most famous guest at her resort was undoubtedly Julia Roberts. Ms. Roberts visited the Isle of Pines in 1984 at the age of 16½ as part of a canoe trip based out of Camp Birchwood in LaPorte, WI. Just eight years later Julia would become a Hollywood star when she headlined in *Steel Magnolias* and *Pretty Woman*, which garnered her two Academy Award nominations.

ABOVE: Julia Roberts (far left) visited Knife Lake when she was 16 ½ years old

ABOVE: The shoreline of the big island where the Forest
Service employees paused before going into the Winter
Cabin to check on Dorothy

THE END OF AN ERA

RADIO SILENCE

"Knife Lake this is Ely . . . Knife Lake this is Ely." There was no response.

The two-way battery-operated radio on the kitchen table of the Winter Cabin provided Dorothy with a way to communicate with the Kawishiwi District of the U.S. Forest Service in Ely. With a call, she could send out for emergency personnel, arrange for flights in and out of the area, and request items she needed at the resort. Her lists ranged from practical things like batteries to things she had a hankering for, like her favorites: ice cream, roast beef or Cool Whip. She made radio contact with the district nearly every day, but as she wasn't used to having a phone, she'd occasionally miss a day or two. The Forest Service employees didn't worry at first. Maybe she was outside feeding the birds or forgot to replace the radio's batteries. Friday, December 12th, 1986, was one of those days. The staff was concerned, but not alarmed.

No Smoke from the Chimney

The Forest Service office was closed for the weekend, but on Monday morning, December 15th, there was still no answer. On Tuesday, the Forest Service staff really became concerned, as no one had heard from Dorothy in four days. Jim Hinds, a Wilderness Technician, contacted Doug Bohman, a pilot for the USFS, and instructed him to ready the de Havilland Beaver, a ski plane, for a flight to Knife Lake for the following morning. The crew left from the seaplane base. It was cloudy and rainy, sketchy weather for flying, but Doug felt confident and took off with the ski plane over the ice on Shagawa Lake. Jerry Jussila, a portage crewmember that had become quite close to Dorothy was along for the ride in case of a problem. Jerry recalled the events that followed, "Jim Hinds and I and a pilot left Shagawa Lake in the morning to fly in and we got up somewhere over Fall Lake and we ran into kind of a sleet, rainy, freezing rain type of situation. We had to turn back around. We couldn't fly into it. That day was a long day, wondering if everything was OK. Kind of assuming that is was but at the same time the uncertainty of it, it was a long day."

The next morning, they tried again. According to Jerry, "We got up the next morning and flew in. The pilot was concerned then about the amount of ice on Knife Lake. Instead of landing on Knife we landed on Portage Lake which would be on the west end of the [Knife] lake, probably 1½ or 2 miles from Dorothy's. We walked with a chisel because we were real uncertain. Portage Lake I didn't think would be any problem, but Knife Lake—with the depth and moving water—we were concerned about that. So we walked and used an ice chisel checking the depth in front of us. We made it there, no problem. Actually, prior to landing on Portage Lake we had flown over the cabins. We had fresh snow as a result of the freezing rain the day before. It had snowed that night and there was no smoke in the chimney and no tracks in the snow. We, I guess without saying anything between us, we knew there was a problem, or figured there was a problem, which there was. It was a tremendously long hike those two miles from Portage Lake to the island. Then I remember we, we kind of stayed down by the shoreline, not wanting to go to the cabin."

CROSSING THE BAR

Sunset and evening star
And one clear call for me!
And may there be no moaning of the bar,
When I put out to sea,

But such a tide as moving seems asleep,
Too full for sound and foam,
When that which drew from out
the boundless deep
Turns again home.

Twilight and evening bell,
And after that the dark!
And may there be no sadness of farewell,
When I embark;

For tho' from out our bourne
of Time and Place
The flood may bear me far,
I hope to see my Pilot face to face
When I have crossed the bar.

Alfred Tennyson

In Loving Memory Of
Dorothy L. Molter

Born
May 6, 1907

At Rest
December 18, 1986

Services Held At
Hickey Memorial Chapel
4201 West 147th St. — Midlothian, IL
Tuesday, December 23, 1986
At 8:00 P.M.

Officiating
Rev. Arlene Christopherson

Interment
Union Cemetery
New Kensington, Pennsylvania

ABOVE: A pamphlet from Dorothy's memorial service

The team discovered Dorothy's body shortly thereafter. She died of a heart attack; her big ol' heart gave out while she was hauling a load of wood for the barrel stove. At seventy-nine years of age, her life ended, and she was alone when it happened. Some may say that dying alone sounds sad and lonely. Dorothy probably preferred it that way. Her testimony in the documentary *Living in the Boundary Waters* attests to this fact:

"I just feel like I'll just take things as they come. I hate to leave this old world, but still, if you have to you have to. Of course I don't think anybody wants to get older. Yeah, I think I have a lot of nice memories. It's been a good world, I think, so far for me and I think people make their own world. At least a lot of them do. So I'll just take what comes. If it isn't what you want, it's probably something you deserve."

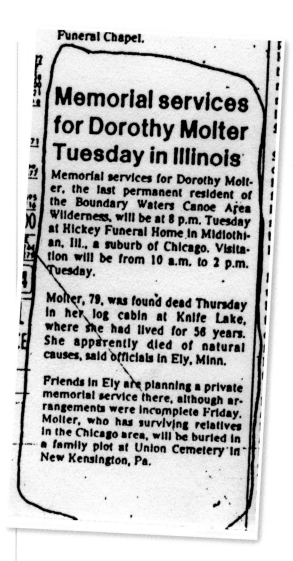

Funeral Chapel.

Memorial services for Dorothy Molter Tuesday in Illinois

Memorial services for Dorothy Molter, the last permanent resident of the Boundary Waters Canoe Area Wilderness, will be at 8 p.m. Tuesday at Hickey Funeral Home in Midlothian, Ill., a suburb of Chicago. Visitation will be from 10 a.m. to 2 p.m. Tuesday.

Molter, 79, was found dead Thursday in her log cabin at Knife Lake, where she had lived for 56 years. She apparently died of natural causes, said officials in Ely, Minn.

Friends in Ely are planning a private memorial service there, although arrangements were incomplete Friday. Molter, who has surviving relatives in the Chicago area, will be buried in a family plot at Union Cemetery in New Kensington, Pa.

ABOVE: Announcement of services in the newspaper

A Time of Mourning

On that sorrowful day on December 18th, 1986, word about the loss of "the Root Beer Lady" spread quickly. A quiet sadness fell over all those whose lives had been touched or inspired by Dorothy. Regional and national media reported her death, and each article tenderly covered the facets of her life that contributed to her celebrated acclaim. Headlines in the papers read:

"Sole Knife Lake resident dies"
  Ely Echo

"Last resident of BWCA dies"
  Duluth News-Tribune & Herald

"Dorothy Molter, last BWCA resident, dies"
  Minneapolis Star and Tribune

"Life Well Lived"
  St. Paul Pioneer Press and Dispatch

"Dorothy Molter: Chicagoan became a legend of woods"
  Chicago Sun-Times

"Nation's 'Loneliest Woman,' Dorothy Molter, is dead at 79"
  New York Times

ABOVE: Steve Molter photographs Dorothy after his last visit with her

Memorial and Funeral

Family in Chicago were notified of her death and a memorial service was soon arranged for the following Tuesday at the Hickey Funeral Home in Midlothian, Illinois with interment at Union Cemetery in New Kensington, Pennsylvania. Dorothy had requested to be laid to rest in the family plot next to her birth mother, Mattie.

The event in Illinois was largely a family gathering, so not many of Dorothy's friends from Ely and Moose Lake were able to make the trip. As they wanted to celebrate her life, many of Dorothy's friends in Ely felt that a service in her honor should be held at her place up on Knife Lake. There was only one problem with this idea—snowmobile use in the BWCA had been banned nearly two years before and a trip to the lake was nearly impossible without them. A group of locals in favor of a trip to Knife Lake, spearheaded by John Rosett, requested that the USFS lift the snowmobile ban for just one day in order to venerate this great woman. Public support for this mission was so great that once again the USFS deviated from protocol and allowed the service. The official Forest Service press release read:

A wilderness setting at Knife Lake will provide the background for a memorial service honoring Dorothy Molter, the last resident of the BWCA who passed away at her remote island home in December. The special service will be held on Saturday, January 10th at 1pm at the Molter cabin northeast of Ely. Special authorization has been given by the USFS to allow snowmobile access in the BWCA Wilderness to the event. An access trail has been marked starting at the Moose Lake landing on the Fernberg Road and at Saganaga landing on the Gunflint side. The snowmobile authorization applies only to the marked trail between the hours of 9am and 4pm on the 10th with no allowance for side trips.

ABOVE: Dorothy's tombstone, which marks her grave in Arnold, Pennsylvania

The Memorial Ride

Peg Rosett, the wife of John Rosett, the organizer of the Memorial Ride, remembers the event well, "After a time, on January 10, 1987, we were able to make a last trip to the Isle of Pines. I have heard various numbers that were on the ride so, between 500 and 1,000 people were able to do this ride. They walked through the cabins one last time and we served donuts and coffee outside just as if she were there. A special memorial service was held by her cabin with people standing down below, very reverently on the ice."

An article published the following day in the *Duluth News-Tribune & Herald* described the scene. Written by Janet Pinkston, it read, "During a brief memorial service, the Rev. Vince Gallinatti of St. Anthony's Catholic Church in Ely said Molter had taken care of people 'with no thought of being rewarded.' And after reading a poem by St. Augustine about how the beauty of creation bears witness to the presence of God, Gallinatti said, 'This is the beauty that Dorothy knew so intimately. This is the beauty in which Dorothy died. She lived as she wanted to live. She lived the life God ordained for her. Her spirit will continue to live on in the memory of those who knew her.' After the crowd recited the Lord's Prayer, there was a moment of silence in which no one made a sound, except for John Rosett, who wept openly for his friend."

TOP: Dorothy's old 1967 Polaris, which great-nephew Steve drove at the memorial ride

MIDDLE: Riders, left to right; Rick Ojala, Pee Wee Maki, Jerome Skraba, Roger Parrott, Steve Molter, John Rosett, Art Knuutti, (clean-up crew after the memorial ride)

BOTTOM: Memorial ride

For those who couldn't attend the memorial ride a small service was held the next day, at the First Lutheran Church in Ely. Over coffee and cake the group of mourners discussed a way in which they could make sure the memory of Dorothy would live on; it was here that the idea of a museum dedicated to Dorothy's memory was first suggested.

One Last Fight

As it turns out, Dorothy's property was the center of one last fight. According to the terms of the agreement that Dorothy had reached with the USFS, when Dorothy ceased residing at the island, the islands were to be returned to their natural state. This meant that no additional facilities could be added, and that existing buildings had to be removed. In fact, the USFS had a Property Disposal Plan already in place, which was approved on the 29th of December, 1986, just eleven days after her death. On January 12th, 1987, Jean Larson, the director of the Ely Chamber of Commerce, contacted the Forest Service about the possibility of salvaging Dorothy's cabins. She inquired on the behalf of a group of "Dorothy's Angels" who hoped to find a way of bringing the cabins to Ely. Coincidently, this was the same day that John Pegors, Regional Director for the Minnesota Pollution Control Agency approved an application for an open burning permit that had been requested by the Kawishiwi District office of the Forest Service. The "angels" needed to move fast, as it looked like the cabins were destined to be burned.

ABOVE: Peg Rosett standing in front of the First Lutheran Church, the location of Dorothy's Memorial Service in Ely

Saving the Cabins

Again, Dorothy's friends campaigned on her behalf as they tried to save the cabins and preserve her memory. The leadership of the city of Ely was actively involved in the process. In a formal letter on January 22, 1987, Ely City Clerk-Treasurer Lee Tessier requested that the Dorothy Molter buildings be preserved so they could be obtained by the city. They would be rebuilt near the Chamber of Commerce at the very visible junction of Sheridan Street and Highway 1. The Forest Service office in Duluth investigated the feasibility and relevance of the request. One resource they consulted was the Minnesota Historical Society. In a letter dated February 4th, 1987, Dennis A. Gimmestad, a Deputy State Historic Preservation Officer emphasized, "Given Dorothy Molter's popularity, we think that all avenues of potential historical significance should be carefully explored before any decision to demolish her homestead is made."

In a letter dated February 26, 1987, the Forest Service granted the request to allow the removal of Dorothy's cabin. The approval came with a few stipulations; the removal was to be completed by April 15th, 1987, and it was to be accomplished without the use of snowmobiles. Previously planned and approved flights would transport work crews to and from Knife Lake. The flights were only to be provided until March 14th, 1987. This meant that Dorothy's Angels had just forty-eight days to remove the cabins, and they weren't just working against the clock; they were fighting the weather as well.

ABOVE: Lee Tessier, photographed outside Ely City Hall

Help from the Voyageur Outward Bound School

Because the crews couldn't use snowmobiles, sled dog teams were the only option for moving such heavy objects. The problem was, not many people know how to drive a dog team. The group needed help, and they found it from the staff and students of the Voyageur Outward Bound School, based in Ely. In a recording done in 2002 as part of an oral history project, Bert Hyde of the Voyageur Outward Bound School described how he got involved in the project, "There's a component of Outward Bound which is service, recognizing that we all need to help each other whether people, animals or plants. We just need to give energy back because we are getting it from somewhere. [When I learned the news of Dorothy's death] we were in the middle of our staff training so I called up Jerry Jussila and asked if there was anything he needed help with. A while later, probably several weeks later, I think it was Jerry, called back up and said somebody wanted to take the cabins down and move them to Ely. [He asked] Do you think you could help do that? I said, well I don't know, how big are the logs? He flew us up there in the Forest Service Beaver to look at the logs. [After looking], I said yeah, we can do that."

The process began with John Rosett and Bob Haapala, who led the volunteer work crews as they dismantled, marked and stacked the logs and assorted pieces of the cabins. (Bud Bujarski, Mort Tuomi, Art Knuutti and Roger Parrott were other men who worked full time on the project.) The Outward Bound crews would then mush up with six-dog teams, load the sleds, spend the night in the Trapper Cabin and then, with rested dogs, make the twelve-mile journey back to the Boy Scout base camp on Moose Lake. The sleds were unloaded and the teams would head back to the islands with empty sleds. This process was repeated night after night until nearly all of the Winter Cabin was removed. Bert Hyde described the work, "In that six weeks I learned more about running a dog team and about maneuvering a sled than I had in the last five or six years before that. It was just amazing, it was fun because you had a trail and you knew where the bad spots were. There were a couple where you were going downhill, on a slant and around a corner at the same time there's a big tree in the way. Yeah, we all moved a ton of stuff, it was nice just to be on a good sled with a good team on a good route."

TOP: Loaded sleds and dogs

MIDDLE: Sled and dogs on the lake

BOTTOM: Outward Bound crew; back row from left to right: Mike Welp, Bert Hyde, Mike Dietzman, John Pierce, Hunter Bell; front row, left to right: Paul Smith, Dale, Bob Mantel

Bad Weather

Unfortunately for the sled dog crews, the weather didn't cooperate. On March 8th, 1987, Minnesota experienced a heat wave across the entire state; the city of Minneapolis set a record high of 73 degrees. The warming trend continued and by the middle of March the route from Knife Lake to Moose Lake began to disintegrate, turning the lakes to slush and portages to mud. The sled dog drivers quickly realized that although these amazing dogs had made a colossal effort, completing the task was no longer attainable. Once again, this dedicated cadre beckoned the USFS to make an exception.

While the sled dog teams had made progress, motorized vehicles were needed to finish the job, but these were forbidden under the terms of the agreement. Almost immediately, community leaders began contacting the Forest Service to see if the plan could be altered. Support came from many different circles; the mayors of Ely and Winton wrote letters to the USFS, as did the presidents of the Ely Igloo Snowmobile Club and the Ely Chamber of Commerce. All highlighted the urgency of the situation and requested the use of snowmobiles and all-terrain vehicles to finish the job.

TOP: John Rosett and Dale share a light moment

MIDDLE: On the lake ice in front of the big island

BOTTOM: Deteriorating trail conditions

Approval is Granted

On March 20th, 1987, in an interagency letter, the Forest Service granted approval to the revised plan. The letter read: "The [USFS] objective is to rehabilitate the wilderness character at her former residence within the wilderness. Cabin removal completion will greatly assist in meeting this objective prior to the 1987 visitor season. You briefed us on the efforts made to remove logs from cabins that are being relocated in the Ely area. Dog sleds have done a portion of the job, but snow and ice conditions prevent further work. Efforts to fund helicopter removal have been unsuccessful, and a military exercise to remove logs by helicopter has not materialized. An alternate action is to allow motorized ATVs for approximately three days to complete the job. Approval is granted for the use of motorized vehicles (ATVs, and snowmobiles/sleds if necessary) under your supervision for the approximate period of time to complete the task."

With that decision an army of about seventy snowmobiles and three-wheelers with any type of trailer hurried to Knife Lake in order to beat the weather and meet time constraints of the USFS's letter, which allowed use for three days. Art and Patty Richter of Ely were involved with the project. "I remember riding in the Beaver [the Forest Service plane] with headphones on. I flew up to help mark the logs," said Patty.

Art recalled, "Bob Haapala called to see if he could use my four-wheeler. It was a 1986 Polaris four-wheeler with two-wheel drive. I was one of the first ones in town to have one. That was the only hitch that didn't break while taking those cabins out. It was Polaris' first four-wheeler so I guess they had overbuilt it."

TOP: A caravan of ATVs hauling the last of Dorothy's cabins

BOTTOM: Roger Parrott assists with a load on Knife Lake

Success

Many hauls were made over the weekend of March 21st and 22nd, and on Monday the 23rd, the last pieces of Dorothy's home of fifty-six years left the island. Bert Hyde summarized the final effort, "That was a real nice conclusion. In earlier years there was animosity between skiers, dogsledders and the snowmachiners. It seemed like doing the whole thing of Dorothy's cabin everybody was involved, and so it didn't matter your personal philosophy of wilderness travel . . . everyone got along together to do the job and we're still friends. I guess that's the part I am most grateful about."

The Peak of Fame

Dorothy's fame reached its peak just after her death when a documentary film about her life premiered. *Living in the Boundary Waters* was created by Judith Hadel Morrisey and Wade Black, and the film's first showing took place on May 22, 1987, at the theater at Ely's Vermilion Community College. Eager to see the anticipated film, attendees overflowed the venue. Hadel Morrisey, a Communications and Arts graduate of the University of Minnesota Duluth, had originally met Dorothy while documenting a three-hundred-mile canoe trip of the voyageur route for the Northern Lakes Girl Scout Council. Working as a freelance video producer and editor in the Twin Cities, Hadel Morrisey collaborated with Black, a documentary filmmaker originally from Alabama, to create the film. Hadel Morrissey and Black made eight trips to the islands, a daunting task considering they had to portage heavy loads of equipment. The final winter trip in March of 1986, taken just nine months before Dorothy died, was the easiest. Hadel Morrissey and Black skied, while dog teams pulled their heavy gear. They stayed for as long as eight days at time, and they visited in different seasons, allowing them to gather plenty of material for the forty-two minute documentary. The film was very well received; since then, the film has been shown dozens of times on public television stations, and many copies of the film are purchased each year.

ABOVE: Dorothy with Judith Hadel Morrisey and Wade Black

Afterward

After the cabins were moved, they weren't reconstructed right away. Initially they were held in storage until they could be reconstructed near the Chamber of Commerce, which is located on Sheridan Street, Ely's main street, right in town. As this didn't seem like a fitting location for Dorothy's cabins, other options were considered. In the spring of 1991 it was decided that the John Rozman Memorial Forest, just on the east edge of Ely, was a better, more natural setting. Rozman had been a game warden based out of Winton, Minnesota, during the famed reign of Chief Bill Hanson, and legendary wardens Jack Linklater and "Jake" Jacobson. A noted role model and mentor for youth, in 1950 Rozman had led a group of Ely children to plant the stand of pines that eventually became the memorial forest.

Once again the cabins were moved, after which they were reassembled by volunteers. Rod Loe, Pete Swanson and Leustek Construction donated heavy equipment and time, and the buildings were reassembled in order to house a museum. Finally, on May 6th, 1993, what would have been Dorothy's eighty-sixth birthday, "Dorothy's Angels" celebrated the culmination of six years of labor and toil, with the grand opening of the Dorothy Molter Museum, a permanent monument to the Root Beer Lady of Knife Lake.

TOP: John Rosett posing on the new railings in front of the Winter Cabin

MIDDLE: Museum site

BOTTOM: Ribbon cutting, left to right, Bob Cary, Ross Buffington, Bea Brophey, Steve Molter, Bob Haapala, John Rosett

The Dorothy Molter Museum

Nestled in a quiet grove of pines on the east side of Ely, the museum was established in order to assure that Dorothy's contributions to the world are never forgotten. The museum would not have been possible without the hastily organized committee and volunteers that solicited the Forest Service for permission to dismantle and remove the cabins.

The Dorothy Molter Museum, located on the east end of Ely's Sheridan Street, was formed to preserve and interpret Dorothy's legacy. Excerpts from the documentary *Living in the Boundary Waters* and personally guided tours through both the Winter and the Point cabins are offered daily Memorial Day Weekend through Labor Day Weekend and weekends in September and October. Each year nearly 6,000 visitors make a point to stop in and learn what made Dorothy so famous. Most leave inspired and also refreshed by the museum's own brand of Isle of Pines root beer, which is reminiscent of the kind Dorothy served at Knife Lake. As the museum continues to improve its interpretive programming and facilities the board and staff remain hopeful that her legend will continue on for many decades to come.

TOP: The path leads to the Winter Cabin

MIDDLE: Paddles leading to the Interpretive Center

BOTTOM: A tour in progress at the Point Cabin

The Isle of Pines Today

Following the removal of Dorothy's cabins all the remaining structures on the island were burned. Every piece of evidence was removed, including the nonnative perennials that Dorothy had planted over the years. The islands were returned, as much as possible, to their natural state of wilderness.

To the average paddler, there isn't much evidence that the Isle of Pines were ever inhabited, or that a courageous woman lived here for the last 56 years of her life. There was once a large sign on the island that read: "This is the former homesite of Dorothy Molter. You are welcome to pay your respects, but please, no camping." The sign has since disappeared, but it doesn't matter. There are no legal campsites on the islands and those who knew Dorothy respect the area, sign or not. Other than that, there is little trace of Dorothy's former home. An observant visitor might notice an unusual clearing on the large island, and if one traveled to the north side of the islands, they might notice the oddly placed ribbon rock, or the strange rock piles underwater in between the islands. (These rocks had been used as cribbing underneath the wooden bridges.) If one were lucky, they might spot an odd piece of lumber or a spike that indicated that someone had spent time there, though this is the exception, not the rule.

On average, the USFS now issues 36,000 permits to the BWCA each year, and receives a total of over 200,000 visitors each year. With the immense popularity of the area, management continues to be controversial. Topics such as logging, mining, snowmobiles, motors, expansion, quotas, and even the adjacent landscapes and views all have the potential for creating future conflict and legislation. The controversy aside, the pristine waters, beauty and solitude of the North Woods that were so appealing to Dorothy still continue to draw adventure-seekers and paddlers from around the world.

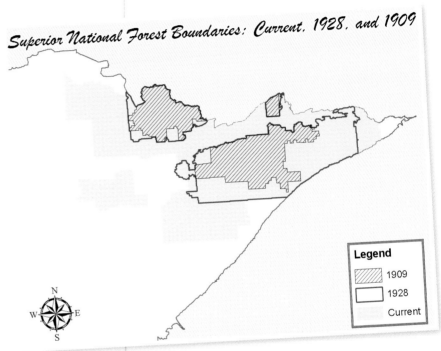

Superior National Forest Boundaries: Current, 1928, and 1909

Legend

- 1909
- 1928
- Current

ABOVE: The boundaries of the Superior National Forest in 1909, 1928 and today

ABOVE: A sign at the Isle of Pines that read: This is the former homesite of Dorothy Molter. You are welcome to pay your respects but please no camping.

ABOVE: Dorothy sitting near one of her cabins

RIGHT: Dorothy Molter, Summer 1986, the
last portrait of Dorothy, which was taken by
Dale Swenson

DOROTHY'S LEGACY

AGAINST THE GRAIN

When Dorothy graduated from high school in 1927, a woman was expected to get married, settle down, and have children. Dorothy knew this wouldn't be the route for her. Later, when she was asked why she never married, she always responded with, "If I ever find a man who can portage heavier loads, chop more wood, or catch more fish, then I'll marry him." Apparently no man ever met her criteria.

An independent thinker from early on, she chose to attend nursing school, which was an act of rebellion in itself. When given the option to stay and work at the resort full-time she again flouted social conventions, even at the disapproval of her family. Dorothy was a model of independent thinking, and her story encourages us to think for ourselves. This is especially true for young women who visit the Dorothy Molter Museum. After they hear about her story, their eyes are opened and they are freer to follow their own path, even if it's not what others would choose for them.

Helping Others

Dorothy's story is also important because it is replete with examples of people helping other people. As the only medical professional in the wilderness, Dorothy helped people and animals alike. Her example teaches us to help when we can, without expecting any compensation, and she taught us that when recompense is offered, to accept it as graciously as possible. In short, she epitomized the biblical imperative "do unto others what you would have them do unto you."

The most important lesson Dorothy leaves us with is to never yield to adversity. Throughout her life in the wilderness, Dorothy faced a diverse array of challenges, from bears that raided cabins to Forest Service letters threatening condemnation. No matter the challenge, she stood her ground and fought for what mattered most. Her resolve and kindness were what endeared her to so many, and these are attributes that don't fade, since they persist in the memories, hearts and minds of those who knew her, and all those who have been affected and changed by her astounding life story.

ABOVE: Danny Galante (left) and Steve Molter knew if anyone ran into trouble or needed help, Dorothy would do her best to help

Perennials

After the cabins were moved to Ely and the Forest Service removed the remaining evidence of her home there, they removed the nonnative plants that had been introduced to the islands. One nonnative perennial remains; each spring the lilacs on Dorothy's islands put forth their small, fragrant lavender flowers. With their deep roots and indomitable spirit, these tough, beautiful flowers are similar to Dorothy—transplants from a different place that are somehow able to survive (and even prosper) amid adversity. Every year in the late spring, the scent of lilacs fills the air, and even today they remain—like Dorothy's spirit—on the Isle of Pines.

ABOVE: Lilacs

Mass Producing Root Beer

Any account of Dorothy's life would be incomplete without her root beer recipe. Given the demand each summer, Dorothy had established a specific routine to make mass quantities of root beer. The process for brewing the root beer went like this. First, Dorothy had to assemble the appropriate equipment. She got out two three-gallon steel tubs of clean lake water and two teakettles of clean water.

She then put the two teakettles and one three-gallon tub on the stove. While waiting for them to boil, she went out to the root beer tent and retrieved six cases of empty bottles, and placed a bench and a bottle capper next to it. She then took out an eight-gallon crock-pot and set it by the bench. In the crock-pot there were stirrers, a ladle, a funnel and a yeast cup. She placed another bench next to this crock-pot. From another tent, she got sugar, yeast, root beer syrup and root beer extract and put it on the bench.

After all the equipment was assembled, she was ready to begin making the root beer. The recipe was simple. The following ingredients were added to the eight-gallon crock: Six pounds of sugar, three-quarters of a cup of root beer syrup, one and a half bottles of root beer extract, four gallons of boiling water.

The mixture was then stirred with an old canoe paddle (pine added additional flavor) until the sugar fully dissolved. Four gallons of cold water were added and stirred into the mixture. The next step involved the yeast. One half-tablespoon of sugar and a teaspoon of yeast were added to a cup of lukewarm water. This was allowed to sit for a minute, and was then added to the crock. Using an old metal funnel and ladle, the bottles were filled about three quarters from the top and capped by hand using an old-fashioned press. The cases of freshly bottled brew were then moved into a tent out of the light to "cure" for a couple of weeks. During that resting period, the yeast would feed off of the sugar. The by-product of this process was carbon dioxide, the cause of all that wonderful fizz associated with ice-cold soda pop!

Need an 8 gal crock (do not use aluminum)
Add * 6# sugar
     * 3/4 cup root beer syrup.
     * 1½ bottle root beer extract
     * 4 gal boiling water
Stir with canoe paddle (pine for flavor)
to dissolve sugar.
Add * 4 gal cold water and stir.

In a cup of lukewarm water add ½ spoon
of sugar and ¼ tsp. yeast stir slow and
let sit one minute — add to crock + stir.

Fill bottles 3/4 way to top, cap and let
sit at room temp at least 2 wks
no sun light.

The original recipe from

from 1976 to 1986 made aprox
50,000 bottles!

Stev Molter

ABOVE: Dorothy's recipe for eight gallons of root beer, as recorded by Steve Molter, Dorothy's great-nephew

Dorothy's Root Beer Recipe (as shared by her great-nephew Steve)

Equipment

Spoon
Bowls
A 1-gallon glass jar

Ingredients

2 cups sugar
2 tablespoons root beer extract
1 teaspoon yeast
½ cup warm water

Instructions

Mix the root beer extract and sugar together in a bowl. In a separate bowl stir yeast slowly into warm water and let sit for a minute to dissolve. Combine the yeast-water mixture with the root beer extract and sugar mixture. Stir well. Put all ingredients in a gallon jar and fill to the top with warm water. Let jar set on a counter, uncapped, for 6 hours. Then, place the cap on the gallon jar and refrigerate for at least 24 hours. It will be ready to drink. It tastes even better if it sits longer.

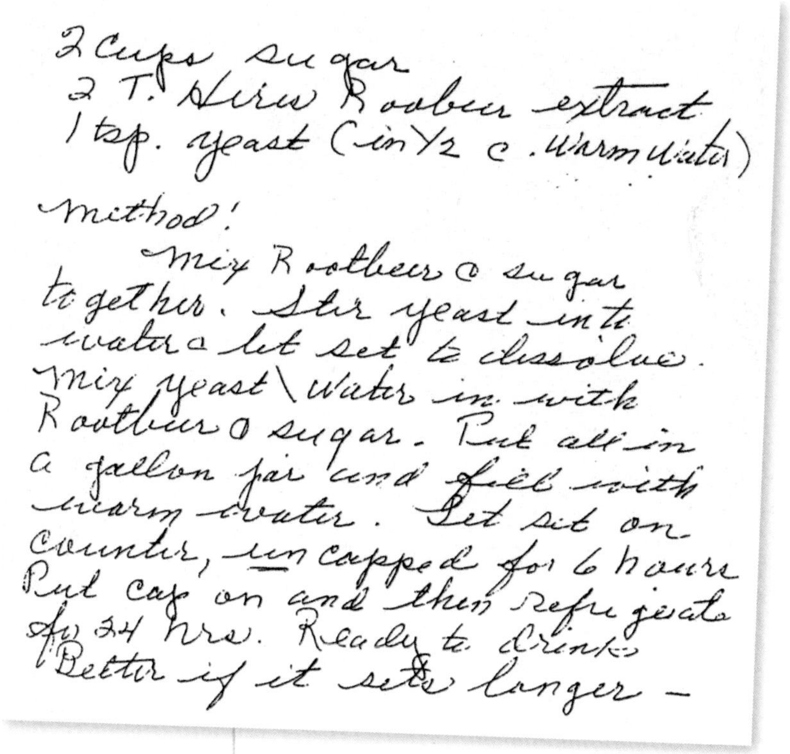

2 Cups sugar
2 T. Hires Rootbeer extract
1 tsp. yeast (in ½ c. Warm water)

Method:
Mix Rootbeer & sugar together. Stir yeast into water & let set to dissolve. Mix yeast\water in with Rootbeer & sugar. Put all in a gallon jar and fill with warm water. Let set on counter, uncapped for 6 hours Put cap on and then refrigerate for 24 hrs. Ready to drink. Better if it sets longer –

ABOVE: Dorothy's recipe for one gallon of root beer

Dorothy's Christmas Letters

When the autumn leaves had faded and the last of the deer hunters had made their final visits for the season, a quiet transition took place on the Isle of Pines. The shortening days and the impassable lake conditions meant that Dorothy was almost entirely isolated; this time provided a much-needed respite for the only remaining occupant of the Isle of the Pines.

It was during these precious moments of solitude that Dorothy took time to reflect upon the events of the previous year and write her annual Christmas letter, which she sent to her resort guests, friends and family. It's easy to picture her sitting at the kitchen table with an oatmeal cookie and a cup of hot coffee in hand, the room lit by a Coleman lantern, its soft constant hissing interrupted only occasionally by the sound of a crackling fire in the wood stove.

Most Christmas letters were written in the third person with help from her "friends"— Louie the Loon, Pilly the Pileated Woodpecker, Baldy the Eagle, Hummy the Hummingbird, or Harry the Woodpecker and Mr. Downy (his cohort). These animal friends not only helped Dorothy teach others (as the letters often featured discussions about the particular animal protagonists), but they also demonstrated Dorothy's childlike ability to find joy in the sights and surroundings of nature.

Extensive excerpts of her Christmas letters are included here, as there's no better way to introduce you to the true voice, sounds and sentiments of Dorothy Molter.

Dear Friends,   December 1955

I wish you could see this "Winter Wonderland" today! The woods are simply beautiful in their fresh blanket of snow. There was another heavy snowfall last night, and the snow is clinging to the trees—everything is so white and beautiful. The branches of the trees are bent nearly straight down from the weight of the snow. The last heavy snow we had was even more severe than this. Seventeen small and medium sized trees on my island were broken down from the weight of the snow. I just finished sawing away at them and cleaning up the mess. They were mostly balsam and spruce trees, and a couple white pines. So far, none have come down under this new snow, but it is still snowing hard and sticking to the trees. Maybe the wind will come up later and blow a lot of the snow off and that will help save the trees.

Dad went to Chicago about the middle of October, so I am all alone again. I will probably go to Chicago for the Christmas Holidays, although I'd much rather stay up here in the woods where I can always depend upon a "White Christmas," and I can see the tracks of "Santa's" deer all over the woods; I was up here in the woods for fifteen years before I saw what a store looked like around Christmas. They have their beauty too, and so do all the neighborhoods with all their gorgeous displays. It's nice to see it all, but I still enjoy Christmas in the woods.

I've been writing so much lately, that I'm just about blue in the face, so I'll skip a lot and just go over the main events of the season. Everything was going along fine until July 3rd, when my tent burned down. It was the one I live in, in the summertime, and call my "Trading Post." It is built for permanent living, with wood floor and walls, and I have a barrel stove for heat in cold weather, and it's as cozy living in there as it is in a cabin, but as soon as the cold weather comes after the fishing season is over, then I move into my Winter Cabin, as most of you know. During the summer months anywhere from twenty to a hundred people a day—sometimes more—stop at my trading post to buy candy, home-made root beer, lemonade, or food supplies, or they just come to visit awhile. As is usual, in times of distress, no one is around. Of course, it's nobody's fault—it's just the way things always happen. So I was alone when the fires started, and I lost just about everything. I did manage to save a lot of small stuff which was not valuable, but otherwise meant much to me. Dad had just finished eating his breakfast, and gone outside somewhere, and I was lingering over my "umpteenth" cup of coffee. I did have some trouble with my kerosene stove when I cooked breakfast but it seemed to be doing all right again, so I put a tea kettle of water on to heat for the dishes. Suddenly the flame shot up, and I turned the burner off right away and tried to smother the fire. The tent was old and I had just had a new tarpaulin put up over it, so it was easy bait for a fire. The flame no sooner hit the tent ceiling when the fire spread like lightning. I used up all the water I had in the tent on the fire, and ran out to carry gallons and gallons more. I called Dad as quick as I could get my breath after toting gallons of water and throwing it on the fire, and soon both of us became fighting firemen of the woods, but not very successful ones. Everybody was out fishing except Cady and Jerry, and we tried to call them, but we couldn't break away from the fire long enough to go after them. Cady soon came over to see what we wanted; then he went back and got Jerry out of bed. Jerry came, but it was too late to save anything—but even if he was there at the time, we couldn't have saved much, because the tent went up that quick. But he was younger than we, and could run faster with water than either of us so he was a big help in keeping the fire from spreading. So, although we lost the tent and most of its contents, we managed to keep the fire from spreading over the island. I can replace a lot of things I had in the tent, but I can't replace the trees or my island, so I thanked the good Lord that the damage was no worse. I dread the thought of what would have happened if there was any wind that day.

In August, my dog, Peg (I called her Susie), died. She had been sick off and on the past year, and I had her to the vets several times, but nothing more could be done for her, I miss her so much. She was my shadow. If I got out of her sight for five minutes, she was sniffing around and looking for me. When I had to go to town and couldn't take her she would actually be sick until I came back. She could tell I was coming when I was several miles away, and she'd try to tell Dad. Then she'd sit on the dock and wait for me. Then when I got home she'd be so excited. I'd really feel cowardly to leave her—but I always took her along if there was no one around to leave her with. She was eleven years old. I could go on and talk about her all day, but I don't want to bore you—after all, dogs are like kids—there's none like your own.

I had a pet bear cub last summer and he was a lot of fun, and a nuisance, too. I called him "Dennis the Menace" and he was just that. I was glad when he disappeared at the end of the summer for he was beginning to get mean. Micky was my pet mink. I found him in a trap last winter, and his leg was broken, so I kept him till it healed, and then onthrough the

summer. I just turned him loose after the tourist season was over, so he could get ready for winter. I see him quite often. He takes fish from my hand, but he won't let me touch him. I had a pet raccoon for awhile, too, and he was a lot of fun, but my brother took it home with him—it really belonged to his little girl. A fisher has been climbing up the window and stealing the cornbread from the birds. I hope he doesn't come around too often. It keeps me busy enough just making enough cornbread for the birds. Last winter the birds got away with fifty pounds of cornbread, seven pounds of peanut butter, two pounds of nuts, five pounds of suet, numerous cookies, and much bacon rind to nibble on. Mostly the chickadees and nuthatches feed at the window. They are such clean looking birds. Some are black capped chickadees and some Oregon chickadees. Most of the nuthatches are red-breasted, but a few are white-breasted. Sometimes they get along well together, and sometimes they fight like the mischief. Right now a lot of them are hanging on the icicles waiting their turn at the peanut butter. They really go for that in a big way. The lumberjacks, whiskey-jacks or Canada jays, eat a lot, too, but they carry off much more than they eat. I must get busy now and make gumdrop cake so it has a chance to ripen for Christmas. Hope you have a nice holiday season, and I hope you get this letter, too. Every year I get a lot of letters returned to me for better address, but that's the only address I have, so I can't forward the letter. I hope those people don't think I have forgotten them. Kindest regards to one and all and very best wishes for a Merry Christmas, and a prosperous New Year.

Sincerely,
Dorothy

Hi! Merry Christmas!   December 1956

It is so beautiful now, with so much snow on the ground, and the trees are bent over with the weight of the snow more than old Santa Claus is bent over from the weight of his toy sack. Occasionally the sun shines, the snow becomes so colorful, I'm almost tempted to go out and pick up all the "diamonds" that glisten in the snow. The icicles hanging from the roof are alive with birds waiting their turn at the feeding station. Truly, a "Winterland," and a perfect setting for Christmas.

The birds don't seem to mind the cold and snow at all. All day long, from daylight until dark, they fly back and forth, arguing and fighting over the biggest and choicest morsels of food. The weasel is out there too, getting his share of the bird's food. The feeding station is like an open cupboard, set right up against the window, so I can just sit here and write, and watch the birds at the same time. I think, though, that the birds get more of my attention than my writing does. Most of the birds that come to the window are chickadees and nuthatches. The whisky jacks and blue jays would like to come to the window, but I have big chunks of suet tied to the trees for the larger birds. The Pileated Woodpecker is scolding every day so I suppose the jays are using the pileated's nest to hide their food in. The nest is in a white pine near my bedroom, so I don't need any alarm clock in the morning. The birds see to it that I'm awake early. But that doesn't mean that I get up when they do. There are also the downy woodpeckers, hairy woodpeckers, American and arctic three-toed woodpeckers, and the brown creepers, pine siskins, redpolls, crossbills and the red-headed woodpecker, but these birds seem to find enough food in the woods, and do not come to feed at the window. The redpolls are so tiny and colorful; one

wonders how such tiny things can survive these cold winters. But they do, and they always seem to be so cheerful. Every time I see the crossbills, I am reminded of the legend about them. The legend is that while Christ was nailed to the cross, the crossbills came along and tried to save Him. They pulled at the nails until their bills became crossed, and they, the birds, became drenched with Christ's blood, therefore, the name, "red crossbills." I like to hear the various legends. I don't know very many, but I wish I knew how to find more, I think the legends are rather novel and interesting.

The deer come around quite often now, since the lakes froze over. There are tracks everywhere. I see Stinky's tracks, too, but I haven't seen him for a few days. Stinky is my pet mink. A couple of boys found him swimming in the lake early this spring and they thought he was drowning, so they picked him up with their landing net, and wrapped him in their coats and brought him home to me. Gee, he was a cute little mite. I figured he was only about two weeks old. He wasn't as big as a chipmunk; I raised him with a medicine dropper. He soon learned to feed himself. I started off feeding him milk, then bread and milk—but he wouldn't eat the bread unless it was broken up very small and soaked in the milk. He wouldn't eat the crusts. Soon he graduated to minnows, and it kept all of us busy catching minnows for him. Gradually his diet consisted of liver, hamburger, large fish, cooked and raw meats, fried and fresh fish, frogs, crabs and eggs. He wasn't too fond of eggs, but he ate them when he was small. I kept him in a cage, and kept a big square dishpan of water in it for him. I had to use something big for his water, for he kept spilling the smaller containers. When we'd get fresh minnows, we'd put them in this pan of water, and it as fun to watch him sneaking up on them and catching them. I sort of envied him all the fun he was having. We had his cage fixed up with a hollow log, a swing, a rubber ball, some tiny bells on a string, tied to the top of his cage, and a sleeping box. He played with these things all day long. It was so much fun watching him I often wonder how I got my work done. I'd pick him up and he'd climb around my neck, then crawl down my blouse, and run around my waist in circles, then stick his head out through an opening, then duck back and start all over again. I guess he thought that was a lot of fun. As he grew older, his toe nails grew sharper, and as a result, I am still wearing scars on my anatomy in memory of his many races inside my shirt. He'd play like a kitten and playfully bite my fingers. He'd never bite hard. We took lots of movies of him in his playful moods. Afterward, I'd take him out of the cage every night and bring him in the house. I had papers on the floor for him, scattered here and there, and it didn't take him long to learn what the papers were for. So I had him almost housebroken. I let him run around in the house for several hours every evening and he really went to town, snooping in all corners. He took great joy in climbing into my magazine cupboard, and pushing all the magazines on the floor. Then he found his way to the table, and it was almost impossible for me to write letters while he was on the loose. He'd push all my writing material on the floor, then try to take my pen or pencil from my hand, then he'd climb on my shoulder to get hold of my nose. Although he wouldn't bite hard, my poor big nose was more tender than my fingers, so I'd have to attract his attention elsewhere. When he'd get tired, he would climb into the magazine cupboard and crawl on a stack of magazines under the radio, and sleep for a while. He didn't sleep long though, and soon all the magazines were on the floor again. The first few nights, I let him stay in the house at night. I was always waking up, hearing something fall on the floor. I had flowers in the house and he thought it was a lot of fun dumping the vases and watching the water run all over the table and my writing material. I eventually had to pull all the chairs away from the table so he could not get up there. So what does he do? I'm standing by the heater, and he climbs up my leg to my shoulder, and then leaps to the table. The oilcloth on the table was a little bit slippery for him, and often he'd land on some papers and slide right off the table with them. He was a lot of fun and a lot of company. When the weather began to get bad, I decided to let him go, so he could get ready for winter. At first he didn't seem to care for his freedom. He'd get out of the cage, circle it a few times, and then he'd climb in again. The first couple of days, he stayed close to his cage. After that, he snooped all around the island; then he ventured into the lake. I think he has made his winter home under the wood pile, for I see lots of tracks there.

The little weasel comes in on the porch every night now, and sometimes during the day. I have a big piece of suet on the floor for him and he feasts on that. He doesn't bother anything else, so I let him come and go as he pleases. He is so small he can squeeze in under the door. The only way I can keep him out is to put something in front of the door, but as long as he does no harm, I'll just leave him alone. There is enough suet for him to feed on all winter, and he makes enough noise getting at it.

I had my hands full for a while this summer. When I had "Stinky," I also had Vera. I got them both about the same time and had to feed both of them with the medicine dropper. Vera was about ten days old. She was a crow; I had to feed her oftener than the mink. It took a lot of my time, but I had a lot of fun raising them. After my sister and her grandchildren came, they helped with the feeding, and there were other children around from time to time, and they all took a hand in feeding my "family," so it wasn't too much of a task. Stinky was cute—Vera was funny. We got more laughs out of her when we fed her. She not only gulped her food down, but she made so much noise doing it, we couldn't help laughing at her. One day shortly after we got her, a couple of boys were feeding her and she grabbed the medicine dropper, and gulped it down. She made some noises that scared the boys so they came and told us. We thought they were only kidding us, but I thought I better find out for sure. I wedged her mouth open, but I couldn't see any sign of it, so I got a long pair of tweezers, and felt around for it. I felt something soft, but I couldn't tell if it was Vera's anatomy or not. I didn't want to pull anything till I knew for sure what I had a hold of. So I felt around some more and finally felt the glass, but it was hard to hold onto. So was the rubber bulb, but I finally got it out. It was some time afterward till she could make any noise, and she looked so silly, I almost think she wanted to say "thank you" in her crow language. We were sure glad when she learned to eat by herself, but even after she was fully grown she expected someone to feed her. One day we heard the robin scolding like the mischief. The robins had a nest in a tree near the tent, and were busy feeding the young ones. We went out and when we heard the commotion we saw Vera perched on a limb near the nest with her head held back and her mouth wide open, waiting for the robin to feed her, and the robins continued to scold her. As she grew older, she became a kleptomaniac. She'd carry off clothespins, bottle caps, papers, dish rags, nails and anything else she took a fancy to.

One day my sister couldn't find her teeth. We hunted all over for them. She thought that Dad and my Uncle might have hidden them from her as a joke. So we thought we'd await results. I went about my work hanging out clothes, and watching Vera so she wouldn't get away with my clothespins. Suddenly I saw her with a strange object in her mouth, and she looked mighty strange, too. I moved closer to her and soon discovered that she had Ruth's teeth. I called Ruth and immediately I was sorry I didn't run in and get my movie camera before I called her, for I sure would have liked to have a movie of Ruth extracting the teeth from Vera. Finally Vera gave in, in disgust, and then proceeded to pick all the flowers out of the vases I had in my rock garden, and then tipped the vases over. Never a dull moment! Vera was a long time learning to fly. When I got her she had a broken wing. She had fallen out of her nest, and some campers brought her to me. Late in the summer she would fly short distances—just around the tent. One day Ruth and I went across to a nearby island to pick some blueberries. We hardly got started when we noticed a crow flying over our heads. It moved wherever we moved, and we soon discovered it was Vera. It was her first "short" long flight. We talked to her, and then she came down from the tree and took turns perching on our shoulders, and eating our blueberries. She became such a pest that our berry picking that day was slow, but we finally got enough for several pies. Vera was a lot of company, even if she was pesky. She would perch on our shoulders while we did the laundry, but we had to watch her after we hung out the clothes, for unlike Stinky, she was not housebroken. Occasionally she would get in the boat, and wait for a ride. I got quite a few movies of her too, but alas, none with her wearing dentures. After she learned to fly, she'd fly to the big island where my Winter Cabin is, and I think the other crows over there were trying to teach her crow life and habits, and to prepare for migration. I could hear them carry on and scold at various intervals during the day when Vera was over there. She knew her name all right, for wherever she was, she would always come when I called her. Her real name was Vera Tick. We named her that after the boys who gave her to us. They had portaged into Knife Lake via Vera Lake when the going was rather tough, and the wood ticks were at their best. Therefore: Vera Tick.

When Ruth's grandchildren came up, they named her Shadow, and they named the mink Stinky. Vera answered to both names. Along early in September, my worries about Vera's future were over. Rodger and Bobby came over with a dead crow in their hands, and I knew right away that it was Vera. A hawk ended her career before anyone could get out and save her. I buried her by the rose bush. Stinky missed her for a while, too. They had become pretty good pals. Vera would go over to his cage many times a day, and they would talk to each other in their own languages. I wanted to keep Stinky, but I was worried as to what to do with him when I went to Chicago. I couldn't keep him caged up while I was gone, and it might be inconvenient for me to take him with me. So I decided to let him go. I'm a little bit sorry that I let him go, for I think it would have been all right to take him to Chicago. He was not hard to take care of. The only thing is that if I put his cage outside, the dogs would scare him, and then he'd smell up the place. It wouldn't be right to keep him in the house all the time. He wouldn't smell up the house unless someone would scare him. I wonder if I will have any pets next year. So far, I have had several mink, several crows, a bear, a screech owl, several beaver, a rabbit, a weasel and several small injured birds—some lived—some died.

More and more people are coming here every year on camping trips. Entire families are getting the camping "bug" pretty strong. I meet people from all over the world. Most of them are exchange students. I have had the pleasure of meeting people from Canada, Germany, France, Spain, Italy, Scotland, Sweden, Iceland, South Africa, Brazil, Mexico, India, Columbia, Australia, China, and a few other places. It certainly is interesting talking to them and hearing about their countries. I wish we could have more time to visit with each other.

The bear made his usual raids on the campers this summer, and there were a great variety of bear stories told. I saw fresh moose tracks by Vera and Portage Lakes. I hope I see it this winter. Occasionally, while hiking, I'd find things here and there that the bear had carried off and ruined. The campers usually turn their canoes over at night, and pile their cooking equipment and lots of cans on top of it, so they can hear the bear when he comes around and dumps it over. Then they try to scare him away.

One night, or two be exact, it was one o'clock in the morning. I was coming home from town and struggling across the last portage with my packsack on my back and five gallon gas can in each hand. It was plenty dark, so I kept my eyes on the ground, watching the trail for rocks so I wouldn't stumble. I could just barely make out the trail. Just as I got to the end of the portage, I looked up too late, and stumbled over something in the trail, and it wasn't a rock. Down I went, and the impact caused the loudest noise and commotion I have ever heard. I swear it was heard clear to Denver. Then a voice yelled "bear!"

I knew then that I had stumbled over someone's canoe. Well then, everything was quiet again so the 'voice' must have crawled deeper down in the sleeping bag and everyone else did the same, for no one ventured forth to scare the "bear" away, I felt about myself for bruises, and finding none, I gathered up my stuff and went grumbling down to the boat, muttering a few choice words about people who leave their canoes right in the middle of the trail. The 'voice' must have decided I wasn't a bear after all, for he came out half dressed and half awake, and apologized. A few of the others hobbled out in their sleeping bags, and we sat around and chatted a while, then the 'voice' being half dressed, went back across the portage with me and helped me carry the rest of my belongings across. A few more words, then I went off for home. They were very nice fellows, but gosh, what a place to leave a canoe! It must have been their first camping trip, or they would have known better.

Sincere good wishes for the very best of Holiday Seasons. May your pleasures be many, and your troubles be few, and Good Health, Good Luck, and Prosperity too.

Yours truly,
Dorothy

Dear Friends,
December 1957

As usual, there is plenty of snow as I am about to put up my little Christmas tree. I always put one up and even if no one else sees it but me. It's so cheerful to have around, and just as much company as the birds. I leave it up until I come back from Chicago in January or February and there is nothing like it to cheer a fellow up after a long hard hike up from Moose Lake on snowshoes.

Last year, Charlie Steward of the East St. Louis Journal, came back with me. He wanted to write a little story for his paper on how ice is put up—the hard way; the way it was put up years ago, before Frigidaires were heard of. Well, he got plenty of experience, both putting up ice, and snowshoeing. A lot of snow has fallen since I was away, so it was pretty tough breaking a new snowshoe trail from Moose Lake to Knife Lake. We took turns breaking trail, and pulling the toboggan, and occasionally taking a Five (the lumberjack phrase for a brief rest interval). When we got to the end of Sucker Lake, we knew it would be way after dark when we arrived at Knife Lake. I didn't want to find myself on rotten ice or around open water in the dark so we decided it would be best to pull in at Prairie Portage and stay there the night. I was glad we did for it was really tough going the rest of the way. It took us six hours to get to Knife from Prairie when generally it takes but three to four hours. Knife Lake never looked so good to me. We could feel the water under the snow, but the snow was too deep, so we didn't get our snowshoes wet. It didn't take us long to get the fire going and get the cabin heated up and get something to eat. We spent the next few days cleaning the snow off the cabin roofs and tent and boathouse. Then there was the water hole

to be opened up, and we tramped trails from cabin to cabin and other trails around where we needed to walk every day. The trails would freeze up during the night so we could walk around with out the snowshoes. Then we got supplies from the root cellar, and I had to make more cornbread for the birds.

The biggest job was cleaning off the snow around the icehouse. That took us a couple of days—not full days. We just shoveled till we got tired, then called it a day. There was thirty inches of snow on the ice slides, and on the lake near the shore. After we shoveled out a few yards, the snow wasn't quite so deep, but deep enough. We knew when we finished shoveling that we had arms better suited for holding a book or a newspaper, rather than for shoveling snow. After the snow was cleared away, we spent the next three days cutting the ice. Charlie did the sawing, and I pulled the ice out of the lake, and up the slide and into the icehouse. It was all hard work, and we took our time and quit when we got tired. By the time the ice was all out, Charlie's time was running out. It was getting dark before I could get all the ice inside, so we just pulled it close to the shore and up on the snow so it wouldn't freeze in if the water came up on the lake while we were in town. We called it a good day's work. The sawing is a hard job, as we had to do it with a hand saw. The power saw is always on the blink by the time ice cutting time rolls around. The other part of the work is hard, too, but it's easier for me to lift than saw. But I was slow with my end of the job, so we had about thirty-six blocks of ice left on the shore to be put in the icehouse. I put the moss in as I put each new tier in, so that slowed me up. But it didn't matter. As long as the ice was cut, I knew I could get it inside. We left the next day for Moose Lake, and it was much easier going back than it was coming up, but we felt good, because we had the satisfaction of knowing that the ice was as good as all in, and we could look forward now to a good rest when we got to town. Charlie was glad to get in the car and sit down. I think he has been sitting ever since. I stayed in town a few days, then had a good trip back. That is, I had a good trip back after I left Prairie Portage. I get that far, and a good healthy snowstorm caught up with me, and the visibility became so poor that I had to turn off at Prairie, and stay there till the storm blew over. That was two days. I expected to have trouble snowshoeing, but it was just cold enough to make good going, and the snow had blown off the lake quite a bit. I could even see our old trail, so I took it, and made it back in three and a half hours. I saw a deer, fox, wolf, fisher and two mink. I took it easy around home for a few days then went back to the icehouse. I got all the ice put in, but I had to shovel it out from under the snow. There was nearly as much snow to shovel as there was when Charlie came up—only I didn't have to shovel over such a large space. After the ice was all in, I found I needed fifteen more blocks and put them in, and was darned glad I didn't need fifty more. I rested up a few days, then went back and put the rest of the moss in, then put the door back on and called it a day—till it's time to start the job over again next year.

It seems like after the ice is up, then spring comes fast. In March the snow begins to settle, and thaw, and freeze again and there is beginning to be a little more sunshine. You can easily see the days are getting longer. There seems to be more game around. By April, the snow is beginning to disappear from the hillsides exposed to the sun. As soon as bare ground appears, the birds begin to come back. Before I have noticed when they got back, I have found the Merganser's nest in the boathouse again, and a black mallard nest on the hill near the bridge. Then the trappers come along, if the season is open.

As soon as the water opens up along shore, we have our bird concerts all day long and the frog concerts all night long. Just as soon as the water opens up a little bit more, our friend, the loon, puts in an appearance, and gives the rest of the woodland creatures some pretty good competition. I'm always watching for the arrival of the spring birds, and check them off in my book as each different kind puts in his appearance. I was cleaning the little cabin one day in late April, and heard a sound I hadn't heard before yet this spring. It sounded more human than like a bird, but that didn't necessarily mean so much because often in the spring the seagulls have some cries that sound pretty human, and so do the ravens. It wasn't quite time for the loons to appear, but I thought one might have rushed the season a little bit. The smaller lakes had enough open water for the loons by this time, but not Knife Lake. I listened, but didn't hear the sound any more, so I continued with my work. I heard this sound again, but couldn't make it out. I went outside to hear it more clearly, but the wind was so strong and noisy, I couldn't hear well. It seemed that whenever I was inside, I could hear it, and the more I heard it, the more human it sounded. I became concerned, thinking it possible that someone just might be out there on the lake somewhere, or in it. The ice was pretty rotten for anyone to venture forth on, and if there was anyone on the ice, he must have fallen in. I got my binoculars, and went around the island twice, looking up and down the shore and all over the ice. I didn't see any holes that were not in the ice before, and they were all too small for anyone to have fallen through. All I could see on the lake was a couple of seagulls, and I watched and listened. Next time I heard the sound it seemed to come from a different direction than where the seagulls were. I went back to the cabin and was just about to enter, when I heard it again. I went behind the cabin out of the wind, and waited and listened and this time I heard it fairly clear—at least clear enough so it sounded like someone calling for help. I looked in the direction, but couldn't see anyone, but they could be right around the point—just beyond my vision. I was petrified for a second. I was scared someone had fallen in the lake. Then I thought it might be Hollis with the mail and wanted a boat or rather a canoe so he could get across. But I was more certain that it wasn't him. I made wild dash for the tent island, where I had a canoe turned over on the dock. As I said before, the wind made so much noise it was hard to hear, so I flopped the canoe on the ice, making as much noise as possible, so he would know I was coming anyway. That is, if there really was someone out there. The last time I listened, I thought I heard my name but couldn't be sure. I've heard loons make all sorts of cries, but I never yet heard one say "Dorothy," so I was pretty sure it was not a loon that I heard. The ice by the tent dock was sinking and there was about eight inches of water on top but I waded in anyway, and it held my weight so I hung onto the canoe and pulled it along with me for safety. If the ice gave way, I could get in the canoe. After a few yards, there was less water, but plenty of slush, and it was hard pulling the canoe through it. Well, maybe not hard, but tiresome bending over the canoe. It was warm work, but I needed the heat as I had no sweater or coat on. I ran out just like I was: thin blouse, thin jeans, and tennis shoes. I didn't know what was ahead of me or what to expect, so I hurried out as I was. My feet soon got cold, and pretty soon they were numb, but I didn't mind that.

After I got out a little ways, I thought it was too darned quiet, so I called, and right away got an answer. I never was so glad in my life to see anyone alive as I was when I got around the point and saw the young man standing on shore and not even wet. I was so scared it might be worse. The only thing wrong was that he couldn't get across the lake without the help of a canoe. He had walked all the way from Ensign Lake; maybe further, so let's just call him Hoofer, to make writing easier. After I got my breath, I found a fairly good place to put the canoe in the water.

I was afraid I might lose the binoculars if I left them in the canoe, as somehow, we might manage to tip it, so I took them out and put them around my neck. I walked as close to the shore as I dared. There were cracks and holes all over the ice, so after I thought I had a pretty good footing I gave the canoe a big shove, intending to put in close enough for Hoofer to reach. But the canoe only went a couple of inches ahead and I went several feet down.

And there I had my first swim of the season. The sheet of ice I was standing on broke loose and down I went. I was going to crawl in the canoe, but it was so close to shore and I was soaked anyway, and besides, "Hoofer" was ready in case I needed help, so there was no need to be so scared. I had been expecting the ice to foul up so I wasn't surprised, or scared. But afterwards, Hoofer said that I had a funny look on my face. I was not aware of a funny look, but if it was so, then I might have been thinking of my binoculars. I know at the time, I was thinking I'd have been better off to leave them in the canoe. But I didn't lose them. They just got good and wet. The situation was funny though, after we knew everything was all right. We got back to the island without mishap, and I got into dry clothes right away, and the cabin was nice and warm. I wasn't cold, but my feet were still cold. However, as soon as I got the shoes changed, it didn't take long to get them warm. That was the biggest relief I have ever had in my life, I think when I saw "Hoofer" safe and sound on shore, when I had visions of him with his head sticking up through the ice, or even worse. I was so afraid he might be in real trouble and I wouldn't be able to help him. But all is well that ends well.

I would have been pretty scared if the ice gave way while I as out in the middle of the lake. "Hoofer" had been trapping and couldn't get back to Moose Lake, yet. Although this is game refuge, it was opened up again this year for beaver. So that's how "Hoofer" came to be up here at that time of the year. It gives you a strange feeling to walk out on the ice one day, and three days later row the boat around the same spots where you walked. There was still a lot of ice around, but at least I could row across to the next island. The ice was all gone around here on May 2nd this year, but there was still a mass of it up on the north arm, but that went away the next day, I think.

April and May are beautiful months, with birds migrating, flowers and spring blossoms popping out, fishermen arriving, followed by flies, mosquitoes, wind, rain, sunshine, warm, cold and possibly a few fish. June, July and August are busy months. Campers are swarming into the woods after peace, quiet relaxation, exercise, fun, fish, blueberries, movies and snapshots. The mosquitoes, flies and bears come swarming in after the campers. Quite a few bears this summer, which treated themselves to quite a few tents and packsacks that didn't belong to them. As a result, they fattened up pretty nicely by fall. Every year, they learn more and more where to get the choicest vitamins and never fail to call their relatives to move in with them. One bear portage, they simply sit on a rock on the hill and wait for you to come along with your packs. When you are on your way back for another pack, he's on his way in the woods with the first pack. He has a good station here. He can watch you, and at the same time, he can watch the next portage. So if you do manage to slip by him, he can get a hand-out from the other fellow when the other fellow isn't looking. The bear hates holiday weekends though, because there are so many people on the portages, he can't get near the packsacks. Therefore, he has to go hungry a few days. Then is he ever glad to see the next fellow come along after the holiday rush is over!

May you have good health and happiness throughout the year, and for many years to come.

Sincerely,
Dorothy

Dear Friends,   December 1958

It is a real blustery day. Just listen to that wind howling in the pines, and look how the trees are swaying. It's on days like this that I don't like to be walking in the woods—I never know when a tree might fall in my path. The windows are all frosty, and big, long icicles are hanging down from the roof. Trees are weighted down with snow, and the weather man has promised us more snow. It looks real Christmassy out. It's too cold and blustery to take a walk, so I'll just sit inside and enjoy the warmth of the stove, and have a little visit with you. We'll have coffee and a snack while we visit. Here is yours. Use sugar? No, no cream either? Well, I like mine black, too. When I'm alone I usually drink tea, but I'm the biggest coffee drinker in the world when I have someone to drink with. Let me know if I bore you. I'll try to talk only of the things that might interest you the most.

Our first real taste of winter came from the Thanksgiving Holidays. It started off with heavy winds, blowing down trees, and with blowing and drifting snow, accompanied by our first subzero weather. The small lakes and ponds froze up around November 16th. When this cold wave came, the big lakes couldn't take it, so they began to freeze up, too. By December 2nd, as far as I know, all the big lakes were frozen over. At least they were frozen as far as anyone could see. More snow came right away, and this I didn't like, but of course, I couldn't do anything about it. I like to see the lakes freeze real good for a week or more before the snow comes, then there is less water on the ice, and makes for better walking or snowshoeing.

I had started out about a week before Christmas, but it was too warm and the snow was so sticky I had trouble pulling the toboggan. Seed Lake was a mess, and hard going again—so much water on the ice. I couldn't tell half the time if I was walking on the ice or in the lake. I finally got across and on through Melon Lake and to Carp Lake. I started across Carp Lake, and it appeared to be no better than Seed Lake, and I knew I would have trouble going on, so I turned back. I left the toboggan on Melon Portage, and came on home to wait for colder weather to freeze up some of the water on the ice. A few days later, Hollis and Arlan came up with the snow sled. They thought they would give me a ride to Moose Lake, and save me that long walk, a very beautiful thought. But wait—what happens? They get within a couple of hundred feet from the cabin, and the sled breaks down.

About the same time I was ready to leave Chicago to come back to Knife Lake, I developed pneumonia. It was the first time in my life I was ever sick except for the usual childhood complaints. I couldn't get anything fancy to brag about later, either. It had to be just plain, old fashioned pneumonia. So I didn't get back home until March. I always catch a cold when I go to Chicago, and usually they are dillies. This cold I was just over and beginning to feel good again, when pneumonia set in—I guess that's what I get for leaving this good, pure, fresh air of Knife Lake.

The ice went out early this year—earlier than I have ever known it to go out. That was on April 18th, and fishermen began to arrive right away. This is no time of the year to be tragic, but there was sadness in many homes this Christmas as I won't say much, except, let us bow our heads a moment in memory of Grant and Rudy, whom most of you know were drowned this spring. And my hat is off to all their friends who worked so hard and defied the miserable weather to drag for their bodies and found them. The dragging continued for ten days of the most nasty weather anyone would—there was rain, cold, snow, sleet, hail, very strong winds—not only for a day or two, but for nearly the entire ten days—and the men had no thought of giving up. They started shortly after daylight, and came in just before dark, with their clothes frozen on them. Most accidents happen in bad weather, but this happened to be an ideal day. The bad weather came after the tragedy occurred. They were good and careful woodsmen, too. You can't be too careful. Especially in the spring when the water is high, and there are so many floating logs about, and even the small pieces of beaver wood can be dangerous, so you early fishermen want to look out for them, and keep in mind all the boat safety rules. No matter how well you can swim, that water is bitter cold in the spring, and you can get a cramp very quickly. Wear your life jacket especially in the spring. A good life jacket—tied on—is good for keeping you afloat for forty-eight hours, so don't panic if you should have an accident, which I hope you never do. Accidents happen to the best of us, so be prepared, even though you do feel safe enough.

This fall, after Dad left for Chicago, I stayed in town a week and . . . took several sight seeing trips with Pat's Dad and Mother. One trip we went part way out the Echo Trail, as far as Weaver's Resort on Big Lake, and stopped here and there looking for rocks and driftwood. One thing, in this country, you don't have to go far to find a rock. The next trip we took was along the north shore to Gooseberry Falls and Split Rock lighthouse, and along the Baptism River. I had never seen any

of these places before, so it was a beautiful trip for me. We had a picnic lunch along the shore of Lake Superior, had time to stop here and there to look for agates. We found some nice ones, too. Although I didn't find as many as the others did, I had fun looking for them. It was all something new to me. I hope when you drive up next year, you will take time to stop and see the falls and the lighthouse, if you have never been there before. It is so much more interesting to stop and visit these places, than to just drive by and look. You don't see so much of the beauty of them, just driving by.

How about some more coffee, and some cake, or another sandwich? I'm trying to take off a little weight, but am not very successful. It takes me three weeks to lose one pound, and I gain three pounds in that many days. I can't win.

The day before I left to go to Chicago, we were heading toward the portage when we saw a flock of seagulls bunched up in water. We wondered what it was all about, for at this time of year, we don't see many gulls. When we got closer, we saw a deer swimming across the lake, with the gulls following it. A couple of ravens were flying overhead. We could see that the deer was hurt. At first we thought that some hunter might have injured it, but it was too early for hunting season, and I didn't know of anybody being in the woods. The deer was headed for my island, so we followed it over. It couldn't swim very well and we could see it seemed to be fighting for life. By the time it got to the island it was almost done for. We saw then how badly it was hurt. The wolves had attacked it and almost tore its leg off. It was broken, and disjointed at the hip, and just barely hanging on. The skin was torn from its whole rump. I debated about coming back for the rifle, and putting it out of its misery, but we were pressed for time and wanted to get going before the wind came up, and besides, I didn't think it would live more than an hour at the most, so we left it there. After we left, we could see the sea gulls coming back. They must have been picking at the deer while he was still alive, for when I came back from town the deer had tried to swim away, but only got a few feet. He must have taken to the water again to get away from the gulls. When you see what the wolves do, you can't blame them for opening up a hunting season. At least man is more merciful in getting his deer. I often find deer killed by the wolves, and often heard wolves howl, followed by a deer bawling but this is the first time I almost came in contact with the actual killing. I followed the deer trail up in the woods a ways to see if there was another deer, but I didn't have time to go very far, so I never found out. But I did see a wolf trail come clear down to the waters edge, alongside the deer, so it must have ran back in the woods when we came along.

Let's have some more coffee, and . . . It's cooling off now, so I better throw in another Yule log. The wind has gone down, and so has the thermometer. It's 22 below now and will be much colder by morning. It was 37 below the other night . . . It's still a little bit early for it to be that cold. That usually comes the latter part of December, and in January.

Quite cold, compared to that night last summer when I had to paddle home all the way from Birch Lake, near Prairie Portage. My motor conked out, or I could smell rubber burning, and heard a sizzling sound like sparks in the motor. In fact, I was just getting into Birch Lake, and then it went bad. I had a notion to stay at Prairie Portage for the night, but I thought everybody there might be in bed. I'm about the only one, in

sixteen continents, who keeps such late hours. It was a nice moonlit night, and very little wind, just nice for paddling, and I didn't mind it at all. It was three o'clock in the morning when I got home. It didn't take long to paddle up Birch Lake, but I had eight trips to make on all the portages. When I got to the last portage, I just made three trips across, and left the rest of the stuff on the other side to come back for in the morning.

I just took the food across and a couple packsacks full of candy across to cheat the bear out of it, if he should come along during my absence. I had a boat on this side of the portage, so I put the packs in and rowed the boat home. It's on these late trips, that I miss my dog. No matter how late I would get home, she would be on the dock waiting for me.

It was nice talking to you. Do come again, and I hope you have the very nicest holiday season ever. God bless you, and come again.

Sincerely,
Dorothy and Cap

From the perspective of Mr. Pilly, the Woodpecker . . .

Hi Everybody!   December 1959

Remember me? I'm the pileated woodpecker who lives in a tall white pine tree right outside Dorothy's window, and I'm the fellow who pounds on the trees every morning at the crack of dawn, and wakes up the neighbors for miles around. Dorothy calls me Mr. Pilly, but the books have a lot of names for me, like Lord God woodpecker, Great God woodpecker, Cock of the woods.

[I'm called] Woodcock, Log cock, Great black woodpecker, Wood hen, Game cock, and maybe a few other names. Woodcock is not proper though, for I am entirely different from the real woodcock. The people I wake up at dawn have special names for me that you don't see in the bird books, or even in the dictionary, for that matter. I have lots of fun chiseling holes in Dorothy's nice big pine trees. She has some real nice big white pines and Norway pines which she is very fond of. So am I. She doesn't like the way I go around pecking big holes in her trees, but I'm such a handsome fellow, and I am a lot of company for her in winter—summer, too, so she has to overlook my bad habits. Anyhow, I make up for my bad habits in the spring when my wife and I raise a family in a tree near the cabin. That pleases her.

Believe it or not, I am as big as a crow. I am very handsome, if I do say so, myself. If you have never seen me before, then look me up in the bird book. I am mostly black, and have a white stripe on the sides of my neck which disappear under my wings somewhere. I have a beautiful red head with a red crest. Those are the predominating colors. If you could see me closer, you might see a tiny bit of yellow, that is very pale to my eye, and I have some grey coloring. My wife is handsome like me, too, except that she doesn't have as much red on her head as I do. Some people mistake us for the Red-headed woodpecker, but he's much smaller than us, and quite different, too, although he has the same colors. At one time we were in danger of becoming extinct because people hunted us for food. Then when the forests were logged, and when fires burned over the woods, we had to find somewhere else to go or else. We like green forests and virgin timber, and there are not many places to find them now, but the forests are growing up good again, so we have a pretty good chance now. I have a lot of cousins, too. They live in different parts of the country. So people call them by many names: the Ivory-billed woodpecker, the Eastern pileated woodpecker, the Southern pileated, the Western pileated, the Florida pileated and the Northern pileated. I am the Northern variety. All of us look pretty much alike, but in different localities, the coloring differs somewhat, and the size varies. The Ivory Bill is the largest of all woodpeckers, and I'm next to the largest.

I have my troubles in this world, too. One spring when I was first married, after my wife and I had our home all nice and cozy, we went on a short honeymoon. When we came back, to our dismay, a pair of flickers had invaded our home, and took complete possession. I was pretty mad at them and I scolded and threatened and did everything I could think of to chase them away, but nothing doing. Then Mrs. Flicker said she was expecting the stork pretty quick—so I couldn't turn her out then. After that, we became friendly, and I'd watch her nest while she was out. Then when the kids were born, she invited me over to see them. My gosh! Such homely things! I wouldn't have the nerve to show them off to the neighbors, but I guess she was pretty proud of them anyway. I sort of felt sorry for the ugly things, so I kind of babysat with them when their parents were out—that is, I would keep my eyes on them. In a few days they had some flimsy clothes on, and they looked a little bit better, but I was really surprised a week or so later, to see how handsome they grew up to be.

Another time a golden-eye duck took my home over. At least that is what Dorothy thinks it was. There were some pale green eggs in the nest, and they were as big as hen's eggs, almost. I got mad and threw them out of the nest. I had to get the nest cleaned out pretty quick, because the stork was catching up with my wife, and we had no time to build another home. Shortly after we got it cleaned up, my wife called me, and showed the kids to me. Talk about homely! How could such a handsome pair as us have such homely kids? I felt badly about it, but my wife said they would outgrow it. I was doubtful, but it turned out she was right. They grew up to be just as handsome as us, and that is saying a lot. I was real proud of them. I taught them how to make big holes in Dorothy's nice big trees, and how to build homes, and where to dig for ants. They became as expert as I am. Later in the summer we visited other bird homes, and most all the kids were homely. Some of the bird parents had twins, triplets, quads, quints, and more, but the smaller birds average four. The ducks usually have from seven to twenty—depending on what kind of duck it is. The duck kids are not as homely as our kids, because they were

born with some clothes on because they have to get swimming almost right away. I know now why we smaller birds sit on our young ones for a few days after they are born. The bird books say we do it to keep the kids warm and to protect them, but from my own experience, I'd say we do it to keep the neighbors from seeing how homely our kids are. We can show them off later, after they get dressed up a little. We pileated are pretty noisy in the spring, but after the kids grow up, we are mostly quiet. When we are chiseling high up in the trees, it's a safe bet we are making a nest, or we are after the funny kind of worms that bore inside the trees. When we peck at the base of the trees, we are after ants. It's surprising how many ants are inside those trees, even though the trees are not dead. Dorothy usually leaves a couple of dead trees standing for us to peck away at, but we like the live trees better. We live mostly on ants and tree worms, and occasionally we eat a few wild berries. I think I mentioned that our bills have a chisel-like end which is why we can pull such big chips out of the trees. Our tongues are long, and the ends of them are kind of speared, so we can spear the ants and the worms as we work. I don't think men have a chisel mouth or a spear in their tongues, for in winter I see them with homemade or manufactured chisels and spears to cut through the ice with, and catch fish. I'm pretty noisy, too. I can be heard for a mile away and sometimes more. In the spring when I'm looking for a wife, I pound on dead trees or something that can be heard far away. Dorothy has some metal boats that I like to pound on for the noise carries pretty good. The flicker likes to pound on them too. Pileated woodpeckers each have our own territory, so we are widely scattered. Our homes might be half a mile apart, or two miles apart. If it is especially good feeding grounds, then we move in closer to each other. That's about all I can say for myself now. You can read more about me in the bird books if you are interested enough. I generally have twins or triplets.

Now, I will tell you something about Dorothy. Right now she is typing her Christmas letter, and making a mess of it. I bet she will have to copy it over. Oh! I forgot to mention that I was one of the candidates for the Minnesota state bird. The Goldfinch was the state bird, and I think he still is, but it's not official. We would like to have a different bird, because the Goldfinch already is state bird for a least three other states besides Minnesota. The last I heard, the school kids were going to vote for the state bird. I think the ten leading birds were scarlet tanager, belted kingfisher, mourning dove, killdeer, pileated woodpecker, flicker, wood duck, and rose-breasted grosbeak, and the loon. The scarlet tanager won out, by a great majority, with the rose-breasted grosbeak coming in second place. Dorothy likes all the birds, but she thinks they should choose a bird that is here the year around—like me. She would like to see me get the honor—either me, or the loon. The loon is not here the year around, but he is most typical. A lot can be said about him, in his favor, but the main thing is that since the state is pretty much of a vacation land, and because of it thousands of lakes, and wooded areas, the loon is most outstanding. He arrives in the spring before the ice is out, and he stays till the day before it freezes. He is such an unusual bird, and is great entertainment for vacationers, who have never seen or heard of a loon before. The people call each other a crazy loon, but how many of them actually know what a loon is? I think if the voters studied the birds more, they would vote for their worth, rather than their beauty. It's pretty hard to find a bird that stays the year round in all parts of the state. Like me—I'm a year round bird in the northern parts, but I doubt

if anyone see us in the southern parts of the state. The cedar waxwing is a year round bird in the southern part of the state, but not up north. So there are many things to consider. I don't know what place I came in when the school kids last voted, but I'm sure I didn't do so well. How could I, when the scarlet tanager got more than two-thirds of all the votes—or close to that many, any way. He is a very beautiful bird and I don't blame the kids for voting for him. But I hardly ever see him up here. He might be around the towns and farms, but not in the woods, at least not in the vicinity.

Dorothy came back to the woods the first of February, or the sixth, to be exact. It was 46 below in Winton that morning. By the time they had breakfast, and umpteen cups of coffee, it warmed up to 26 below zero. It was a nice crisp morning to ride in an open air snow-traveler. Lloyd and Walt and Hollis went along. Things went fine till they got out on the lake, then Dorothy's snow-crawler acted up and after Hollis had spent considerable time with it, they decided to abandon it and double up on Lloyd's sled. They had quite a big load, and it was slow going, but better than walking. On Ensign Lake, the game wardens flew over, and landed. They had a short social visit, and then the plane went on. I guess in three minutes they were flying over Knife Lake and it took the sleds several hours to struggle on. But they finally made it just before dark. We birds go to bed pretty early, but I heard them coming, and soon I smelled the coffee, and supper cooking. I was glad to see her back. Some company came several times while she was gone, so I didn't get too lonesome. Besides, there were the chickadees to keep me company, and the nuthatches, whiskey-jacks, blue jays, downy woodpeckers, and a few others, besides a few animals. A lot of men have these snow travelers, and wind sleds now, so

Dorothy had visitors come up nearly every week end to do some ice fishing. They caught a few fish, too. As soon as Dorothy got back, she had to go around cleaning the snow off the cabin roofs and off the tents. Then put snowshoes on and tramp trails around the island so the snow would freeze hard enough to walk on. Then she had to get supplies from the root cellar.

The bird feeder was about empty, so she filled it and made more cornbread for the birds. The birds get lots of nice suet, peanut butter, cornbread, nuts, and cookies. I don't like any of that stuff, so I leave it all to the other birds. The partridge and spruce hens won't eat anything Dorothy puts out, so she puts gravel under the cabin for them and they are hanging around here all the time. She tried corn, and chicken feed for them too, but they said, "No, thanks." In the summer time, the spruce hen, or spruce grouse, will eat blueberries out of Dorothy's hand, but nothing else.

There were lots of pretty birds around last summer, and it was the first time Dorothy saw the Cape May warbler here. She likes the Blackburnian warbler and the Harris sparrow, because it isn't everybody who gets a chance to see them, and they are very pretty. They are not uncommon birds, but at a glance they are mistaken for others, and people just don't notice their markings. A pair of Evening Grosbeaks spent a good part of the summer around her tent, but she never could find their nest. This is the first she has seen them around for about six years. The woods were just full of beautiful bird songs this summer. I don't sing myself, but I have other ways of letting the world know I am around. Me, and the flicker, with our big mouth, and our hammering on the trees and waking people up at dawn! The humming bird was around Dorothy's flowers all

summer, too, but she could never find their nest either. Most of the birds go south in the winter, except the woodpeckers, and jays and some finches, and Crossbills. The Loon is about the very last to leave. I saw him near the boat house one evening. Next day the lake froze up, so I often wonder if he made it out O.K. He and his wife had twins last spring and Dorothy got some pretty good movies of them on the nest and in the water. They sure put on a good show for her. The loon kids are born with some clothes on so they are not as homely as mine. They go for a swim as soon as they hatch. It's fun watching them. Boy, if you think I'm noisy, you should hear him. I don't think he ever sleeps.

Old Bruno Bear will be glad to see summer again for he likes to pester the campers. There was one real friendly Bruno here this past summer. Several boys on their first camping trip stopped to rest down around Moose or Newfound Lake somewhere. They saw a nice modern looking campsite so stopped there for their rest. They never saw such an elaborate campsite before, so they looked around at the nice table, and then some distance away, they saw the powder room and nearby was a garbage disposal unit. The heard a commotion in the garbage pit, so they looked into it, and saw old Bruno marooned there. Looking back toward the lake they saw a canoe coming so they told the occupants of the canoe what was going on, so the young fellows landed their canoe, and everyone got their heads together to find a way to free Bruno, and get some pictures of him. So they got rope and made lassos, and they swung true over Bruno's head and arm. Then the boys backed up and tied the ropes to trees, and then while they got cameras set, one of the boys placed a long pole in the pit for the bear to climb out. Old Bruno seemed to know what it was for, as he came tearing out of there lickety-split, and growling like a husband whose wife just ran the new car into a telephone pole. The bear took for the tall timber, and the boys for the wide open spaces, cameras flying in the air. I never found out which ones were scared the most. The bear took a liking to the boys, or at least it seems that way, for every camp they picked out, old Bruno was there in time to eat. When they reached Knife Lake, and had a visit from the bear that night, that did it. They broke camp, and came down to Dorothy's place and got a cabin for the night. Dorothy told them that Bruno might show up here too. So they put the hook on the door and felt pretty safe. Well, in a reasonable time they heard a knock at the door, and then a banging clatter of tin cans and smelled the aroma of garbage. Bruno was right on schedule making his rounds. That was enough camping for the fellows. Next day they took off for the safety of their home towns. That was the night Bruno interrupted a card game in Dorothy's tent. She scared him off that night, but the following night he brushed against the door and the cards went flying in mid air. A few minutes later he was in the supply tent, but I've told you about that. Dorothy likes to see bears, but when it gets so that they can't mind their own business, then, the jig is up. I don't think our heroes will lasso any more bears, but I think they are a year younger now, since the bear scared them out of a year's growth.

Dorothy would like to write more, but she might get some company today. If so, she will send this out to the printer, so she can have the letters out for Christmas. I have enjoyed watching her write this, and I'm sure she wants you to have a nice holiday season, so I will get in my two cents' worth too, and say "A Very Merry Christmas, and a Very Happy New Year

to all of you, and the very best of health." I must go and pound on a few trees now, so if company comes, I can annoy them. Good-bye, now, and best of luck to all.

Sincerely,
Mr. Pilly Woodpecker,
Dorothy and Cap

From the perspective of the White Wing Crossbill . . .

Merry Christmas Everybody, December 1960

It's that time of the year again. Goodness, where did the time go? This is me, the white wing crossbill. Some people think I am a freak of nature, because my bill is crossed. I'm not a freak. My bill is crossed for a purpose. I'm a beautiful bird, and I live most of the year on Dorothy's island. Some years there are not many pine cones, so I have to move on somewhere else where they are more plentiful. My cousin, the American crossbill lives here, too. We usually travel around in small flocks, and flit around high in the tree tops. Sometimes we come to the ground and find something to eat. It's pretty hard to see us in the trees, but we show up good on the grounds and add color to the objects around us. We have a weak sounding voice, something like the peep of a canary. We sound very pleasing when all our voices blend together. We are not afraid, and when we are on the ground, anyone can approach us, and see how our bills are crossed. We are mostly a rosy color, with black wings, and we have two wide white wing bars. Sometimes you can see a few dark stripes on our backs. Our tails are rather short, and forked. Our wives are very different. They are a greenish or olive color with lots of yellow. They also have the wing bars. Our cousins, the American crossbills are much deeper red, and they don't have any wing bars. They have some red blended into their wings. Our kids are different, too. For several months,

they are mottled with a mess of difference colors—brown, different shades of red, orange, yellow. They look like someone put different color paints on a spoon, then flipped the spoon and let the colors fall where they would. But the kids look pretty in their first clothes. The young females are mottled with yellow and olive, and their back stripes show up more. Our bills are very strong and we use them to open the pine cones. We can even break off strong twigs with our bills.

Dorothy never saw young crossbills before, so I gave her a treat this summer and brought my family around. My cousin brought his family, too. We found some nice juicy bugs around the wood pile, and when Dorothy saw us, she gave us some good wild bird seed. She gave us bread crumbs too, but we liked the seeds much better. We came around every day for more, and we ate so much of it, she had to get a few more bags of seed when she went to town. Early in October, we left the ground, and went to the tree tops again. It was time for the kids to learn the art of breaking upon pine cones, and extracting the seeds. Dorothy was going to ask the chickadee to write this letter, but he couldn't stop eating long enough to. Last year the pileated woodpecker did all the talking. Since she fed me and my kids so well this summer, I thought it was only fair that I should do something in return, so I offered to do the job for her. I hope you will like the letter, and I'll try not to make it too long and boresome.

Dorothy's Dad left Knife Lake on October 16th and it's a good thing he did, or he might be here yet, the weather had been so rough. There were a few nice days after that, but they came too late. She likes to see her Dad leave here before the bad weather sets in. Dorothy says the nastiest time of the year, is from the time the leaves are all gone, till about November 15. There may be a little nice weather mixed in now and then, but I wouldn't count on it. During this time we get that damp Chicago weather, and thirty degrees feels more like zero. After the lakes freeze, then zero feels like summer time. But if it's windy, then that's a different story.

Dorothy went to Chicago as usual for the holidays, and also visited different towns in Michigan. [She] caught her usual cold, too. When she came back she stayed in Ely a few days, and took in the winter carnival. That was fun, especially the sawing contest, and the ice fishing contest. It seemed funny to see several thousand cars parked out on the frozen lake, and cars driving back and forth all day. It was a nippy day, too, but everybody was dressed for it. After returning to Knife Lake, the first thing to do was make a fire and thaw out. "Old Smokey" (that's the stove) kicked up a fuss and filled the cabin with smoke. The water hole had to be opened and the wood box filled. That was all for the first day home.

Several times, Cap went exploring for new places to get wood and go into trouble. Sometimes he would get [the snowmobile] stuck in a snowdrift, and sometimes the engine would stall, then he would have to walk home, but it usually happened nearby so he didn't have far to walk. One time Dorothy waited till almost dark, then went out looking for him. She followed his tracks a ways, then they were drifted over and she couldn't tell the fresh tracks from the old ones, so she followed several sets of tracks. They didn't lead to Cap. Then it was too dark to see anymore, so she came back to the cabin and got a flashlight, and a walking stick, and went off in a different direction to look. This didn't do much good, so she came back again and tried all over again.

Once, while she stood, thinking what to do next, she thought she heard a call, so she headed toward the sound. She didn't hear the sound any more, but she kept going anyway. After walking quite a way, she stopped to rest. Then she thought she heard the faint sound of crunching on the crusty snow. She listened good, and once in a while she heard it again, but couldn't see anything. She went on a little farther then called out, and got an answer, so she knew the crunching sound was not an animal—or was it? There were fresh wolf tracks in the snow in several places she noticed when she flashed the light once in a while. Anyhow, the voice was human, and she soon caught up with her Dad. As usual, he had trouble getting the motor started, and to make matters worse, somehow, he managed to let the engine catch fire. So he was stranded and had to walk home. He was using a shovel for a cane, so Dorothy gave him her stick, and the flashlight, and they headed home. Dorothy walked ahead and tramped down the snow as she went along to make it easier for Cap, but it didn't help much. If she had known he was so far away, she would have come back for the snowshoes—but that would not have helped her Dad any, for he can't walk with snowshoes. It was only a mile, but it was the longest mile either of them ever walked. It took an hour and a half to get home. Ordinarily, twenty minutes would do the trick. They were both too bushed to play their usual games of pinochle when they got back.

The next trip to Moose Lake, Dorothy walked. She saw fresh Moose tracks on Portage Lake, and various other places nearby. Early in June several early fishermen saw two moose swimming across Knife Lake, near Dorothy's Point Cabin. They went out in the boat to get a closer look, and were so excited they forgot their cameras. They said it looked like a couple of barges, going across the lake.

The bears behaved pretty well this summer. They should, because they had lots of fish and blueberries. It was a wonderful year for the blueberries. Just after Dorothy's brother and sister left, she was walking across Carp Portage, and near the other end some one in a boat called out to her and asked her who her friend was that was following her. She looked around, and there was Bruno, only a few yards away, trying to look innocent. They both stood still and tried to out stare each other. Neither one would give in. I don't know which one of them would have won out, but some newcomers came across the portage then, and distracted their attention. They made four trips back and forth on the portage, and each time the bear was by a bush watching his chance to help them carry a packsack. On the final trip across, as I mentioned before, it was a wonderful year for blueberries. It was a mad race to see who got to them first—the bear or the campers. Dorothy beat the bear at this end of the lake, but she had no time to go farther up the lake for more. While picking blueberries this summer, she found a nighthawk's nest—if you can call it a nest. The eggs lay on a bare rock. She saw the bird first, and knew by the actions that there was a nest nearby. So she looked for it. She knew it would be hard to find. So she spent a good hour looking for it. Every time she reached a certain spot, the bird got excited, so Dorothy concentrated all her attention to that spot. She walked back and forth, back and forth, covering every inch of ground. The nighthawk tried to lead her away, but Dorothy ignored her. Even Mr. Nighthawk came around to help the Mrs., but it was no use, and Dorothy kept right on looking for the eggs or young ones. Finally she stood still and tried to think things out, and as she stood there, she thought she heard a very weak little peep. It was such a weak sound that she thought she might just have imagined it. She looked down and listened again, and there at her feet was some old, old deer droppings. As she continued to look, she saw a broken egg shell among them. She bent to pick it up and there she saw an unbroken egg. She had to look at it several times before she realized it was really an egg. It was colored so much like the droppings that it was hard to tell which was which. About a foot farther away, she saw a cattail down, and wondered how that got way up there. She couldn't see any plant life around that it might have come from, and she kept looking at it and trying to figure it out, then she saw a tiny black eye. She stopped and took a blade of grass and touched the fuzzy thing lightly with it. It moved, and as it did so, it let out a frightened, scarcely audible peep. Dorothy was satisfied now that she found the prize. She got some good movies of Mrs. Nighthawk trying to get her away from the "nest." Two days later, the other egg hatched out, and the parents found another hiding place for the kids. But Dorothy didn't bother to look for the new home. The nighthawks just have two eggs. We crossbills have three to four and occasionally five. They are a pretty bluish-green, and dark spots on them. They are easy enough to see if you can find my nest. This year my wife and I had four kids—three girls and a boy. We'll be looking for some more of Dorothy's bird seed next summer, and in the spring. Right now we are stuffing ourselves with pine cone seeds. She wants to thank everyone for all the nice letters and cards and calendars she received last Christmas. There are so many to write to, and its hard to get around to everybody, so to those who didn't get a letter she wants to thank you very, very much, and she hopes you will enjoy this little missive; so do I. We would all like to wish you the very best Christmas ever, and the best of good health and good fortune to all of you. God bless each, and everyone.

Sincerely,
Cap and Dorothy

From the perspective of Louie the Loon . . .

Hello Everybody,

December 1961

This is me—Louie, the Loon. I arrived on Knife Lake last April, while the lake was still nearly all covered with ice. I had lots of fun at that time sticking my head up through the holes in the ice to watch Dorothy chopping wood, or carrying water for cleaning the cabins. I've kept my eyes open all summer, so I wouldn't miss anything that goes on around here. It sure gets pretty active around here at times. Between the campers and us birds, it gets pretty noisy. But I guess I'm the loudest one of all, and I swear, sometimes the campers would like to tie my mouth shut for a while. You can hear me, all day long and all night, too. A little loss of sleep doesn't hurt me any—I'd just as soon stay awake and yell my head off—well, not off, but you know what I mean.

I had a very pleasant surprise this summer—I was selected the official state bird of Minnesota. Dorothy and I are very pleased about it. The Goldfinch was just a stand-in until they could discover something that would be more appropriate for this type of country—you know the idea—mainly vacation land, full of woods, lakes, and campgrounds, and plenty of other representatives of Mother Nature. In fact, they thought I was so interesting, they gave me the honor. I'm sure all the campers think I'm a very interesting bird. I don't live all over the United States—only in certain localities. So there are many people who are not acquainted with me. Guess I better tell you a little about myself.

I am a big bird—maybe as big as a goose. I weigh about eight to ten pounds, average, and stretched out, I average 32 to 38 inches. I mean all my relatives average those numbers. People call us crazy loons, but sometimes I wonder about people. Our plumage is black, marked with white spots on our backs.

We are white underneath. Sometimes in the sunlight our heads and necks take on a greenish or purplish metallic sheen—sort of like the grackles have. In winter we lose our white markings. If you could pick us up, you would find that we feel hard to the touch—not soft and fluffy like the smaller birds. We have short wings, and they are pointed, and sharp on the edges. This enables us to hang onto the slippery fish that I catch. It also serves as a good defense against enemies, too, but I don't know if I have any enemies or not. If so, I don't remember encountering any.

Three of my toes are webbed together, and the hind toe is separate, and flat. We loons are famous for the way we can submerge without any effort, and with hardly a ripple to show where we went under. We are excellent divers, too, and very quick. We like to tease the campers and dive, and come up in some other spot where they are not expecting us. We are good swimmers, too. We can go down more than a hundred feet. We are at home, both on the water, and under the water, but we are absolutely no good on land. Our feet are placed so far back, that we are too unbalanced for walking. We make our nests very close to the water, so we don't have to do any walking. Sometimes the water rises, or the wind washes it over the nests, but that doesn't matter—the eggs will hatch anyway. We don't really build a nest. We just find a little hollow in the middle so the eggs don't roll out. On occasion, when there is nothing better around, we just place a few reeds and a little moss among the rocks along the shore. Usually we have two eggs. They are very large, like a goose egg, maybe. They are an olive-brown color, and are covered with black, or dark brown spots. They hatch in about 29 days. On the same day as they hatch, after the chicks are dry, they take to the water. They learn to swim and dive almost immediately. When we parents think they need a rest, we submerge our backs partly, and let them climb up and ride a while. The young ones are just plain black color. To the casual onlooker, there is no way to tell the male parents from the female. Some authorities claim the female is smaller, but other authorities differ. We cannot take flight from shore. We have to run on the surface of the water a long way, sometimes half a mile or more, before we can take off but once off the water, we rise rapidly, and we fly fast, but we don't fly so high. We usually fly over at about two or three hundred feet high, sometimes higher. On the water and in flight, we burst out with our calls.

We have five or six different calls. Sometimes we sound like we are laughing, sometimes yodeling, sometimes shrieking. Sometimes we sound like a wolf howling or a woman screaming. We have great fun making all kinds of noises. People think we act like maniacs, but I think they act like that themselves sometimes. Anyhow we keep the campers guessing whether we ever sleep or not. We have lots of fun running up and down on the water, laughing and screeching and playing. When someone gets too close to our nest, we put on a great show. We even stand on the water and dance a bit, and yell to

attract the intruders away. Sometimes we have to give an alarm and our husbands come to help us chase the intruders away.

We have various names, besides what the campers call us when we keep them awake. The most popular is the Common Loon. Then there are the following names: Bib Loon, Great Northern Diver, Imbed Diver, Hell Diver, Ember Goose, Walloon, Ring Neck Loon, Black Billed Loon, Guinea Duck and Green Head. I don't know where all the names came from—probably some author had too many names in his notebook and wanted to get rid of some, so he tossed them at me. The only one in the selection that I really like is, Great Northern Diver. It sounds more like me and it gives me a feeling of superiority.

Us Common Loons winter mostly in the Gulf of Mexico. All the loons prefer to winter near salt water. I suppose you are tired of hearing all about me, so let's go and see what Dorothy is up to. I wasn't sure I could write this letter, for I'm not here the year around, but the other day, I saw her pet mink hanging around in the bay by the boat house. He told me lots of things that go on when I'm not around—especially in the winter time, so I guess I can make out O.K. with this. The mink and I don't speak the same language, but we can manage to make ourselves understood pretty well. If I understood him right, he said they had a pretty mild winter last year. Oh, it was cold, and they had snow, but the last couple of winters were not nearly as severe as Northern Minnesota is accustomed to.

In January, Cap and Dorothy went to Michigan to visit relatives. On their way to Gladwin—that's maybe fifty miles or so north of Midland—Cap got sick on the bus, but they managed to get to their destination somehow, and got an ambulance to take Cap to the hospital. He remained in the hospital for about a week, and then they went to a cousin's for several weeks so Cap could recuperate. They managed to do a little visiting before they returned to Chicago. They thought it would not be wise to do any more traveling.

While in Chicago, Dorothy had her eye taken care of. She went to a doctor every other day for over two weeks, and that cut out a lot of visiting, too. Last year, she had a pet squirrel—a very small, baby squirrel. She raised it with a medicine dropper for a short time, until it learned to eat by itself. One day it got behind the stove, and when Dorothy bent over to pick him up, the handle of the water dipper rammed into her eye. She went to town the next day to have it looked after, and she stayed in town several days, till she could use her eye a little. She took Ralph her nephew with her to help on the portages, and perhaps for moral support. Dorothy had her usual canoe load going back to Knife Lake, and managed to fumble and stumble across the portages O.K. but in the first portage, she was fortunate to meet Ray Grunnert of the Canadian Border Lodge, and he and his guests helped her across that portage. Ray is always good about helping Dorothy on the portage whenever they meet. With some of those loads she has, I think they should meet more often. Well anyhow the eye gradually got better. Then toward the end of the year, it began to give her trouble again, and as she was going to Chicago soon anyway, she decided to have it looked after while there. Since then, she has had no more trouble.

The squirrel went to Chicago with Betty, Dorothy's niece. He had a nice train ride, in the baggage car, and amused all the train crew. While he was in Chicago he went to school and amused the kids, and the teachers. He even went to night school. He went to restaurants and ate ice cream out of a dish like the rest of the kids. He was some guy. He slept in a bed, under someone's pillow. In the morning he would go to the kitchen and find his "potty," then sneak back to bed till the rest of the household got up. Then one day the household got up and found the little fellow dead. It was decided the cause of death was probably too much varnish from chewing on the furniture, or else he found some paint or some other tidbits in the basement that was not good for him. There was much mourning in the neighborhood that day.

It was around Groundhog's Day when Dorothy got back to Ely last year. She stayed in town a couple of days, then came up to Knife Lake and got things ready for putting up ice. She shoveled snow around the icehouse and the ice slide, then went out on the lake and shoveled. But before she finished the lake, the water came up and it was useless to shovel anymore. So when the "icemen" came up, they went farther out in the lake and found a good spot to cut where there was no water, so they shoveled that off. Her friends from Two Harbors rigged up a power saw with the old engine for the light generator and it worked pretty good. It didn't take long to get all the ice sawed, but it took some time to get it all in the icehouse. The ice was all pulled up on the snow to keep it from freezing in, till Dorothy or some one could get it in the icehouse. But alas! It froze in anyway. Thus it took longer to get it all in the icehouse. There was lots of help to put up the ice, but the men only had a short time to work. Besides the men from Two Harbors, there was Lloyd and Hollis and Wendell Wilson. Dorothy's brother, Bud came up for a couple weeks—just in time to help put the ice in the icehouse. With all the delays they had, they finally got it all in. But they had to cut more ice, as some had frozen in the flood water so badly they couldn't get it out without breaking the chunks.

This was all new to Bud and he got a bang out of it, and some aching muscles. After Dorothy fell in once, with a chunk of ice, Bud learned the proper way to saw the rows of ice. One day while working on the ice, Dorothy and Bud saw four deer just a couple hundred yards away from them, just watching and playing around the point. So Dorothy and Bud quit working for a couple hours and watched them and followed them and took pictures.

I arrived at Knife Lake on April 26th. I flew over several days before that, and yoo-hooed at Dorothy several times, but the lake was not opened up enough yet, so I had to land on some little lake nearby, which was already opened up. The ducks and seagulls were already here, and so were a lot of other birds. The woods were full of music, day and night. The birds sang during the day, and at night the frog concert was in full swing. Of course I had to get my lungs going too, but no one thought I was very musical. The first fishermen came up on May 3rd, but they didn't get very far up Knife Lake, because of the ice. On May 5th, the first paddle pusher came up. He was paddling alone, and out for three weeks. He had a rough trip up here, and the weather wasn't the best ever, and he was tired out. So Dorothy fixed up a bite to eat, and they ate and gabbed, and got acquainted, and she let him have a small cabin for a few days till the weather got better. He had to break through ice on Moose Lake and a few other places before he reached here, so he got pretty well broken in on a spring vacation. He did pretty

well for the first trip, and for being alone. He camped the full three weeks, and just about half of that time was not exactly weather made to order. Of course after he had to leave, then we had beautiful weather. Isn't that always the way? The ice was nearly all gone on May 6th, but long after that, you could see "icebergs" here and there on the south shores of a few lakes where it was sheltered from the sun. The water rolls down from some little pond or swamp on the hill, and freezes. During the winter this becomes a mass of ice, and from a distance, it looks like a waterfall, with foaming white water. Otter Track Lake is a good place to see these "icebergs." You may see three or four, or more of them there. One year—that long hard winter we had—I forget what year it was—around 1950, I think, when the ice didn't go out till May 30th (Dorothy calls it the year of the two winters), well anyhow that year you could still see these "icebergs" in July.

Dorothy's sister, Helen, came up this June with her two oldest grandsons, and stayed for three weeks to visit and help her out. They were all good helpers too, and Dorothy was glad they could come. They boys had never been up here before, and they sure did like it, and had a wonderful time, and got a thrill in seeing deer and beaver outside of a zoo. Dorothy took them on an overnight camping trip once, and they are still talking about it. They caught a trout, and cooked it over a campfire, with the old stand-by beans, and it made a delicious meal. This was all a new way of living for them. They did a good job putting up the tent, and doing camp chores. After they went back home her sister Ruth and her two oldest grandchildren came. They stayed most of the summer.

Most of you remember Ruth and the kids, Betty and Ralph. They have been here quite a few times, so I guess they must like it here, too. One day Betty and Dorothy saw a cow moose swimming across the lake in Portage Bay, near the beaver house. Dorothy had her movie camera along, and she took some movies of it while it was swimming and when it climbed on shore and stood and shook the water off, and turned to look at the two in the boat, then it ran into the woods. All this time, Dorothy and Betty were within 50 feet of the moose, and getting close up shots. Dorothy has seen many moose, but was never so close to one before. Now after the moose had gone, she looked at the camera and it just dawned on her that there was an exposed film in it, which she had forgotten to change. Of all the dumb things to do, and after all those years in the woods just seeing moose at a distance—oh golly, what's the use of talking about it.

There were just oodles and oodles of those pretty yellow Evening Grosbeaks around this summer—not only on Dorothy's island, but on the campsites, as well. It seems they liked something in the wood ashes. Dorothy never saw so many here before. Usually she sees just one or two pairs, but this year they really took over. It was such a pleasure to watch them as you could approach them within a few feet, and they were not afraid.

And now, it's time for me to go. I'll have to hurry because I think the lake will freeze up tonight, and I have to have open water to take off from. "So long, Dorothy and everybody, I'll see you in the spring, the good Lord willing." I'm pretty quiet this time of year, so excuse me for not yodeling my farewell.

Bye-Bye now. I know it will be too late to wish you Merry Christmas but I hope you had one. Love and best wishes from Louie Loon.

Sincerely,
Cap, Dorothy and Louie

P.S. Well, I hope Louis got off O.K. The lake was all froze over the next day, which was Nov. 28th. But several days later it opened up again and it seemed like it never would freeze over entirely. But finally it froze over on Dec. 10th, the latest it has frozen in years. The government is still after my island and insists they are going to get it. What kind of a country is this? Is a man's home his castle, or isn't it? Anybody got any ideas? Bye, now, and very best wishes to everyone.

Dorothy

From the perspective of Harry the Woodpecker . . .

Hi Everyone,   December 1962

GREETINGS OF THE SEASON. I'm Harry the Woodpecker, and my friend here is Mr. Downy. We both look alike, but I'm much bigger. His measurements from tip of bill to tip of tail are six to seven inches. My measurements are from eight to ten inches. We are both year around residents wherever we are found, and we are very friendly birds. Here, Downy, come close and let the folks see us together. There, how's that? See the difference in size? We are both black, and white. We look like father and son, don't we?

Our backs are white and we have black wings and black tails. Our heads are black and white striped, the colors blending into the colors on both back and wings. Our outer tail feathers are white, and there are white bars and spots on our wings. Both of us have a pretty red spot on the back of our heads. It's about the size of the end of a pencil. The females look just like us, except they do not have the red spot. My bill is very large. We are both very clean looking birds. We are the only woodpeckers that have a white back, so it is easy to recognize us. Our call notes are the same—nothing musical about them; but pleasing to the ear anyway. My call is louder than Downy's.

I prefer living in the woods, but Downy likes both the woods, and the towns. He likes being around people, but I'm more shy. We nest in holes in trees, but he makes a neater nest than I do. His nest is usually gourd shaped, and he lines it with fine chips. I don't bother lining mine, or smoothing the walls. The nest hole is large, and it goes down a foot or more. There are from four to six eggs, white, and glossy, with a rosy appearance. They are thin shelled too, and are laid in May. We have cousins all over the country and some differ in size, and some are lighter or darker, but not too much difference. We have several names, such as Big and Little Sapsucker, Big and Little Guinea Woodpecker, Black and white-trillers, Little Tommy (Downy) and Harry (that's me). We are really not sapsuckers though, and the real sapsucker looks different than us. We eat mostly insects and wild fruits. We sometimes eat cultivated fruits and grains, but a very small percent. We like the wild fruits much better. The farmer blames Downy for spreading poison ivy, because the seeds are his favorite winter food, and after he expels them, they germinate freely. But he does the farmer more good than harm, so . . .

I've told you a lot about us, so look at us close. Come closer, Downy. There, now we will turn our backs and you can try to tell which of us is which. If you are not sure whether I'm a big Downy, or he's a little Hairy, here's how you can be sure. See, my bill is much bigger than Downy's. My outer tail feathers are white—just plain. But look close at his and you will notice a few tiny black bars; only you have to be close to see them. Now look at the red spot on our heads. Pretty, huh? He has just a plain red spot, but if you will notice, mine is divided by a fine black line at the top, then blends together at the bottom. This red spot and my big bill is the easier way to distinguish us—if you can get a close enough look. Otherwise, you just have to judge by our size.

Well, let's join Dorothy in a coffee klatch. You folks have your coffee and snacks, and we will go to work on this bacon rind and peanut butter before the lumberjacks, whisky jack, camp robber (Canada/Gray Jay) gets here. I'll keep right on talking and give you the low-down on Knife Lake activities this past year. Umm, yum-yum! This bacon rind is good. How's the coffee? Gee, it sure is taking the lakes a long time to freeze up this year. There is not much snow yet either. October was a colder month than November. It did snow several times and it froze up, but the snow and ice all went away again, and early in December. Dorothy was going up the lake in the boat. She can't remember ever doing this in December before. Dorothy thinks the winter will be like it was last year—that is long in coming but once here it stayed, and brought too much snow.

Cap was sure glad to be back in the woods again and back in his snow-sled. He sure liked his sled, and was just like a little kid, with a new toy where the sled was concerned. It is a blessing that his health was spared so that he could enjoy his sled each winter. I don't think there was ever anything Cap liked better than the sled, even though sometimes it was pretty rough going. Dorothy always had plenty of wood cut so he could haul it home. She handled the heavier pieces and they worked out a system so he could easily handle the rest of it. The beaver was kind enough to cut a lot of trees down, and Dorothy made use of them—all except the bark and the branches. The beaver didn't want to give those up. So Cap was in his glory, hauling wood.

One time they took a trip to town, intending to bring a big load back but the going was so tough, they had to leave part of their load on the Newfound Portage, and make several trips back and forth to the end of Ensign Lake. Finally they had all the supplies at Ensign Portage, and as it was getting pretty late, they covered everything and left it there, and went on home with just a small load. When they got to Portage Lake, they couldn't see the trail very well, but made it to the next portage, then got hung up between a stump and a tree, and couldn't get out of the mess. They finally gave up and Dorothy hurried on ahead, and walked home and brought back a sled to pull Cap home on. He couldn't walk very good in the snow, and it tired him out so much. It was too much for him to walk home, so Dorothy pulled him on the sled. It pulled real good until they got almost home, then it was really tough. Dorothy could only put about a foot at a time through the slushy parts, and several times Cap got off and tried to walk, but it was too much for him. Dorothy talked him into getting back on the sled, and with time and work, and patience, they got out of the slushy stretch, and the rest of the way was easy. In fact they were home before Cap realized it. He thought we were on the other end of the Island. It was so dark, he couldn't figure out where he was. It was a big relief to know they were right there by the boathouse. They were both bushed, but after some nice hot soup and other food, they felt refreshed, and Cap even felt like playing a game of pinochle. I can't say that Dorothy felt like it, but they played a couple of games. And of course, she lost.

Time was going by pretty fast now, and cabins had to be cleaned; and other work to be done before the fishermen arrived, so both Cap and Dorothy kept busy at something or other. Then they moved to the tent, as the ice was going fast. On May 5th the ice was out, but on May 3rd a couple of fishermen found their way through to Knife Lake. They had to break a little ice here and there to get here, but they made it.

They were just plain glad to get back to the woods again, after being "penned up" all winter.

It was nice to see the fishermen again. Quite a few fishermen were stopping in now and Cap enjoyed talking to them and swapping tall tales. He was feeling fine, and in good spirits, and he was out fishing a little each day. He was happy tinkering around his motors and glad to be living in the tent again. He was looking forward to seeing all the fishermen and campers. On May 7th, he got up at the usual time and went out for a while, then came back and began coughing. Then he said he couldn't get his breath, and before anything could be done, he had passed away. It all happened so quickly. Dorothy had been expecting this for several years, but now that the time came, it was entirely too sudden. Needless to say how she felt. His body was shipped to Chicago for Masonic for Commandeer services. It was a beautiful funeral and so many people to pay their last respects. His family will never be able to thank all those people enough for their kindness and generosity. He certainly would be proud if he could see now how beautiful it was, and all the attention and respect shown him—but maybe he does know. It is hard to say the right things to all these people who came to say their farewells. Just saying our thanks, and that we are forever grateful, is not enough—but what else can we say? But I think you understand.

Freda came back to Knife Lake with Dorothy. When they got back, there was a bowl full of money on the table, and a tablet full of notes that people wrote. There was no one here to help them while Dorothy was gone, so they just helped themselves to the candy, beer, pop and whatever else they needed, then wrote a note, and left the money in the bowl. It sure made

Dorothy feel good to know there are honest people around. Where can you go, and have sixty dollars laying in plain sight and no one around to know the difference, and customers going in and out at leisure, and not bother it?

There was emptiness around Knife Lake without Cap, but there were many campers coming now, and there was lots of work to do, so there was no time for brooding. But Cap will never be forgotten. Dorothy had lots of company. Everyone had a grand time—when Dorothy didn't have them working at something or other. Also over 2700 campers stopped in to make candy purchases, etc., and some stopped for a visit. The coffeepot was on all summer long, almost, and Dorothy enjoyed all these visits.

There was plenty of wildlife around, too. A loon had a nest nearby, but one day some boys found it and picked the eggs opened. That made Dorothy mad, and she told them off, but not that it did any good. One day she and Freda found a seagull with a fishhook in its mouth. It was a sick "bunny" for a while, but soon it ran to the water, and made its escape to a reef nearby. It was there several hours, and other seagulls came to help him. Finally he went elsewhere.

Ruth stayed until October. Before she left, the leaves were all turning and the weatherman gave us a few nice days, so Ruth and Dorothy took advantage of it and took a trip up Otter Track Lake to see her neighbor, Benny. It was a wonderful trip, and a beautiful time of year. They enjoyed their visit, and enjoyed Benny's vegetable garden and flowers. Benny, as usual, was busy hauling rocks, dirt and mulch from miles away. Ray was there, and he showed the "girls" around. They enjoyed themselves so much they stayed for three days. Dorothy doesn't get time to go anywhere very far in the summer, so she really enjoyed this trip. They explored a lot of portages—Bearskin Portage, Plough, Cedar, Esther, Jasper, Monument Portages and others. They took their last swim of the season on October 2nd, and found that the water in Otter Track Lake in October is not exactly steam heated. The swim was brief, but refreshing after all the hill climbing.

Time is flying fast, and soon it will be time to go to Chicago for the holidays. She always leaves us lots of cornbread and other goodies to last us till she gets back. She is busy cutting wood these days for the winter, and writes letters all evening. She said to tell you that she still has some letters from last year that Louie, the Loon wrote, so if you didn't get one, please let her know, and don't forget to send your address. Well, I hear the Whisky Jack (Canada Jay) coming back so I'll fill up some more on this delicious bacon rind before he gets it all. You folks better have more coffee and some of Dorothy's yummy gum drop cake, too. I hope we will see lots of each other next year. I hope everyone will have a very nice holiday season. Good luck, to all, and may God bless you and keep you. We birds, and Dorothy wish you the very best of everything in the years to come. And thank you everyone, for being so good to Dorothy, and us birds.

Cheerio!
From Dorothy, and Harry, the
Hairy Woodpecker

From the perspective of a Blue Canoe Paddle . . .

Dear, dear friends,   December 1963

Well, this is as good a day as any to stay in and write. Such a day. Beautiful, though. It came last night, about twilight, falling on city, field, woods and highway, heaping them up with a silence, deep and white, glittering with diamonds, and tying up traffic—you know what I mean—Snow! And the forecast is for more snow followed by strong men with shovels. Jack Frost is busy painting the windows, and probably by the time you get this Santa will already have been around, and gone back to the North Pole. He was almost late for Christmas, as he had some trouble getting around these lakes because it took them so long to freeze up. Just like last year, the lakes were late freezing up.

You don't know who I am, so here goes. I am a broken paddle. Dorothy found me one day, washed ashore along the rapids. I was broken in two, and beat up some, but she picked me up anyway, and brought me home with her, and put me on a fence with a lot of other broken paddles. She painted each one of us a different color and we look real nice. Each of us will be named after a different boys and girls camp. I am painted a pretty blue. I don't know what shade it is—Dorothy just kept mixing different paints until she got the shade she wanted.

I am named for Camp Mishawaka. Well, I'll tell you more about myself, and these other paddles. There isn't too much to tell. They all came to bad ends caused by bow-men and stern-men who decided to be a little bit rough. All of us have been on many canoe trips, and saw lots of nice country, and met nice camping companions, and saw all kinds of wildlife. Then fate comes along and introduces these rough fellows. I met my end one day when my boss wedged me between a couple of rocks and tried to push the canoe off still another rock in the rapids. I stood the strain as long as I could, finally I had to give up and I just broke in two, and became worthless. It's a good thing these fellows had an extra paddle with them. My pal, Pinky, here, was once shiny and new and proud to go on his first canoe trip. After only two days out, his master slapped him on the water trying to make it sound like a beaver slapping his tail on the water—that is the quickest and surest way to break a paddle, and it is just plain abuse.

Now Greenie, here, has made many trips, clear up Atikokan and back to Ely in round-about ways and he was good for many more trips, but one day someone carelessly laid him on the ground in such a manner that when he dropped his heavy pack on it, the paddle broke. Whitey, there, met his end when his party was having a water fight, using the paddles to splash each other. Orchid met his end when his crew tried to paddle up the rapids, instead of portaging around, or wading up. Red got his when someone tossed him and he landed just right on the rocks. Yellow got his when someone gave him a toss, and he landed in the campfire, unnoticed till it was too late. Occasionally a paddle breaks, merely by the user paddling against the high waves—but this seldom happens, and when it does, the chances are that there was a flaw in the paddle or it had previously been weakened. Most of us were broken through carelessness, though. Blackie was stepped on, and

Grey was used as a baseball bat. Oh, it's amazing to see how many different ways the paddle pushers find to break paddles. Well, I'm glad Dorothy picks us up and paints us. We look nice around her rock garden.

Oh! Look who's here. Gee, it's nice to see you again. Stick around. Look fellows, its Rosie Redpoll. He's a male, but he's so pretty, we call him Rosie. Also, we call the female Rosie, although she is not as bright as the male. Aren't they cute? Just listen to that soft sweet twittering sound. Gee, there must be thirty to that flock. There they go, up in the branches of that birch tree—they are coming over here to the alders. Oh, goody, now we can get a nice close look at them. Stand still now and they will come closer. They are very friendly. Chubby little fellows, aren't they? They resemble goldfinches in size, shape, actions and song. Look, here's a male on the lower branch. See the bright crimson spot on his forehead, and the black under his chin? Those are the best identification marks. He is actually 5½ inches in length. He doesn't look that big, but that is from the tip of the bill to the tip of the tail. He looks so small you wonder how he can survive the winters, but he is used to the cold climates. He was raised in the far north, as far as the Arctic Circle. Look how colorful he is. His back is striped much like a sparrow, but he has lots of pink, too. The stripes or streaks are brownish and buffy on a background of grayish brown. The cheeks and lower part of the throat, the chest and the sides of the breast are deep pink. The rest of the under parts are white. The rump is pink, mixed with grayish-white and streaked. Tail and wings are grayish-brown and dusky. The wings have two dull white wing bars, and the wings are long and pointed. The tail is long, and deeply forked. The bill is small and conical, and sharply pointed. Here are some females.

See, they also have the bright crimson spot on the forehead, and the black chin. But they are duller than the males, and they don't have as much pink on them. Their sides and under parts are white. Notice how all the birds chatter constantly while they feed? Sounds pretty musical, doesn't it?

If you go over by Dorothy's cabin, you will find that she has some nice wild birdseed for you. You think these birds are pretty now—you should see them during nesting time, when their colors are much brighter. They do look very colorful against the snow, don't they? Well, as I said before, they live and breed in the far north, from the sub-arctic to the northern states, and Gulf of St. Lawrence, Northern coastlines, and Great Lakes area. They nest in low trees and bushes, making their nest loosely of small twigs for a foundation, and weaving in grasses, and line with feather, fur, and down. The nest is rather bulky looking outside, but neat and warm inside. There are usually two to six eggs, of a pale bluish-green color, speckled at the larger end with dark brown, and a few black spots. The young birds are brown, buff and grayish, and the forehead is streaked instead of having the red mark. During the nesting season and raising the young, the Redpolls don't have much time for singing—just offering soft twitters and warbles, but after the young are raised, they make up for it and don brighter colors, and sing more melodious than the goldfinch. In winter, they migrate to the Northern states. They always travel in flocks, sometimes two or three hundred in a flock, but most commonly there are about twenty-five to fifty. They usually migrate with the crossbills, and grosbeaks and goldfinches.

Dorothy had lots of other visitors last winter, beside the birds. Almost every weekend someone came with their snow crawler. Twice in March, the snowmobile club in Ely, and Grand Marais, MN, gathered together at Dorothy's. The Ely group encountered "cool" weather (27 below) when they left town, but they had easy going on the lakes. Dorothy had hot soup and coffee for them when they arrived. And everybody ate right out on the lake. The Grand Marais group came the following week, and also had lunch out on the lake. They had nicer weather to start out in, but later it got just warm enough to soften up the snow and make traveling difficult. To add to their troubles, they encountered rain, snow, and sleet. They were slowed up considerably by the slushy snow and arrived in Ely hours behind schedule, and way after dark. [They were] tired, cold, wet and hungry. Dorothy was hoping that everyone refilled their coffee thermos before they left Knife Lake. I'm sure some hot coffee would have gone good by the time they got to Moose Lake. Dorothy thinks a cup of coffee is good any time, anywhere.

Actually, it was a short winter, but a very cold one, which made it seem longer. I was glad to see the first crows on March 22 and the seagulls a few days later then gradually other birds came back. On April 23, the first loon came back. When he comes, then you know it's only a matter of days until the lakes open up for fishing. There were fishermen and trappers here on April 25, but they couldn't get very far up the lake. On April 29, the first paddle pushers came. Thereafter almost every day someone was around.

This was a summer of plenty, and not enough. That is, plenty of campers (Dorothy had over 3,500 visitors between April 25th through October 25th). That does not include the winter visitors. Also there were plenty of mice, squirrels, chipmunks, bears and other pests. Not enough blueberries or rain. There seemed to be plenty of deer and other wildlife. Even the moose showed himself from time to time. There were plenty of fish, and still not enough. You know how the fishing goes. Fishing is usually good yesterday or tomorrow, but not when you go fishing. Really, though, there were some nice fish caught. There are plenty of fish in the lake—nice ones, too, but why the darned things get stubborn and won't bite at times, it's beyond me. You can see them, so you know they are there. Well I suppose they get a lazy streak every so often, just like we do.

Helen and her grandsons were here in June and part of July, then Hazel came for a couple of weeks. Hazel hasn't been here for several years, so it was nice to have her back. Then Ruth came, with her grandchildren and stayed the rest of the summer. Dorothy kept everyone busy. All the kids became experts at washing root beer bottles, and Helen, Ruth and Hazel became experts in the "still" (making root beer). It kept everyone busy trying to keep enough root beer on hand for the thirsty campers. There was a steady stream of campers coming in every day. Bears, Ugh! There was a steady stream of them, too, and all summer long. Dorothy said she guessed every bear must have had three cubs this year, for it seemed that everyone who saw a bear, wherever it was, it had three cubs. At one time during the summer, there were nine bears around here. It kept everyone busy chasing them away, and campers were robbed of food. Good thing Dorothy had some extra supplies on hand. Some campers were discouraged by the bear, and cut their vacations short. It was just impossible to scare the bears away, or rather keep them away. Larry and Lowell spent a whole afternoon chasing bears off Dorothy's island, but next day the bears were right back. One night Steve and Dorothy were walking across the bridge and right there in the middle of the bridge, heading their way was Bruno, with a couple of pesky cubs trailing along. It's just a one way bridge, and I guess Bruno thought he had the right-of-way, but Dorothy had different notions. She clapped her hands and ran toward him, stamping her feet and yelling at him, making all the noise possible, which was a tremendous uproar. I'll bet the space men heard it way up there. Anyhow it brought results. The bear must have thought the Thundering Herd was after him. As far as Dorothy knows, he is still running.

I hope everyone keeps healthy this winter, and many good things come to you. Maybe it's too much to wish you wealth, but wealth doesn't necessarily have to mean money. Dorothy thinks she is wealthy in friends. She sure has plenty of them, and you are one of them, too. Really now, we can't wish you enough good fortune. Thank you so much for listening to all this chatter.

> With kindest regards and very
> best wishes from
> Blue Paddle and Dorothy

From the perspective of Hummy, the Hummingbird . . .

Dear Dears,

December 1964

Hmm—it is such a beautiful, warm, sunshiny day here—just like a day in June—here somewhere in Central America. It makes me feel-so-good, I think I'll just perch on a small branch somewhere near the garden and write Dorothy's annual letter. I know just what to say because I have been getting letters from gossipy little birds up north, and they have kept me posted on all that goes on, since I left there in October. I'll fly over to the garden and see what I can find to eat first, and then I'll come back and get to work.

The chickadees tell me that the lakes up north are all frozen over now, and there is lots of ice and snow, and Dorothy's cabin windows are well frosted over on the porch. But the window by the table (where the feeder is) is all clear, and they can see inside. She is still feeding them peanut butter, suet, bacon, cornbread, bird seed, and nuts. It all sounds so good, but I'm afraid I couldn't very well eat that kind of fare. I need a more delicate diet. Dorothy did not take any trips very far from her place this fall, as the weather was too cold and damp, but she took many walks and climbed just about all the hills around, and she enjoyed walking around the beaver ponds, watching the beaver. She saw a few mink here and there, and lots of deer. She saw moose tracks, heard wolves, and saw many birds. She waded hip deep in water to get pictures of the pitcher plant.

She wanted to get some wild cranberries, but the beaver had the pond flooded too badly. The blue jay says she is out every day sawing a little wood, or taking short walks, and occasionally taking pictures. Pretty soon she will have to spend more time cutting wood, for the weather will be colder from now on.

Gee, I guess it's about time I was telling you who I am. I'm Ruby-throated Hummingbird. Some folks call me Hummy for short. I think most of you are familiar with me. We Hummingbirds are of a very large family, and we differ greatly, but I'm sure most of you know me well, for I am the most common one in North America. I am very small and dainty. In fact the Hummingbirds are the smallest birds in the world. There is a giant hummingbird which is about as big as a common sparrow. He lives in South America. If you think I'm beautiful, you should go to the library, and see some pictures of my South American relations. I don't believe there is a judge living who can pick out the most beautiful one, I won't say this is the most beautiful bird, but it's the one I like to talk about most. That's because he is so small, and don't all of us love the tiny things? This little fellow is called the fairy hummingbird, and he is only 2¼ inches long from tip of bill to tip of tail. He weighs about as much as a dime. I weigh about as much as a penny, maybe a trifle more. I'm about an inch and a half longer than he is. It doesn't sound like much, but if you saw us together, you would think I was a giant. Gosh, wouldn't you love to find a nest of the Fairy? The eggs are the size of a very small navy bean. Ruby's eggs are the size of a large navy bean. The young are the size of a small insect, like a small beetle. The nest is only about the size of a quarter, or very small walnut. The nest cavity is only ¾ inch in diameter. The nest is cup shape, and the cavity opening is about an inch or slightly less, in diameter. A quarter will just cover the cavity. The entire nest is about the size of an English walnut. There are two very small eggs, about the size of a very small navy bean. They are pure white, without any kind of a spot or mark on them.

We arrive in the woods early in the spring just when the first blossoms are about to open, and we stay till late in the fall. We don't mind ordinary cold weather, but we don't like freezing temperatures. We left Dorothy's place early in October, as soon as the flowers faded. We like it at her place as she has some nice red and orange colored flowers for us. Sometimes she holds a red flower in her mouth, and we go over to her, and sip the nectar from it. When it gets too cold, we fly to Florida, and Central America. We fly pretty fast, and we get a good feast before we leave, then we fly all the way across the Gulf of Mexico—non-stop flight, to Yucatan, with nothing more to eat till we reach our destination. That's 500 miles and more, and with a good tail wind, we can make a mile a minute. Don't you think that's pretty good for us little fellows?

Gee, here I've been talking all this time about myself, and I'm supposed to be writing about events at Dorothy's. I don't know much of what goes on in the winter time, but the other winter birds keep me informed so I hope you don't mind some of the second hand information. I heard by the grapevine, that Dorothy spent Christmas and New Year's on Knife Lake last winter. She was only in Chicago two and a half weeks after the middle of January. She had a lot of winter visitors on Knife Lake last year. They came on motorized snow sleds. It was fun having them come in for a coffee klatch. Some came for ice fishing, and some came for the ride and for the mere privilege of being in the woods in the good old winter time. There was

one party of about six or seven adults came up to camp out. They found a campsite close by and set their tent up, and got everything in order. They had all the comforts of home in their tent; even a heater. I guess all they needed was hot running water. Things went well until about one A.M. when everyone awakened, chilled to the bone. No matter how they tried, they couldn't get warm—just kept getting colder instead. The walls of their tent were stiff and white with frost from their breath. After shivering long enough, they discovered their fire was out, and the spare fuel was all gone. So as it was only 30 below zero, they saw Dorothy's light was still on, so they headed for her warm stove, and later heated up a cabin to spend the rest of the night in. Everyone had a good time, though.

Dorothy made her last trip to town via snowmobile in April. The days that followed that were filled with the re-arrangement of dust and cobwebs—that is spring cleaning. The first loon came to Knife Lake on April 27th, and he left on November 28th, just before the lakes froze. He proved to be quite helpful to her this spring when she was out walking in the hills. After walking several hours a heavy fog came up, so Dorothy headed for home. Before too long, all her landmarks were fogged out, so for a while she didn't know just which way to turn, and while thinking things over, she heard the loon call out. She knew it was on Knife Lake, so the rest was easy—she just followed his voice, and soon was on the lake and not far from the boat.

This fall she saw an interesting thing, a falcon killing a seagull. She believes it was the peregrine falcon. Pete first noticed the commotion in the air and he called Dorothy. By the time Ruth and Dorothy got over there, the falcon was on the water's edge, holding the seagull's head under the water. They both struggled for a while, as the gull had the falcon's foot in its mouth, and the falcon struggled to get it out. With his free foot, the falcon held the gull's head under water, till it finally drowned. And with his foot still in the gull's mouth, the falcon hopped along on one foot, dragging the gull uphill on shore, about ten or fifteen feet away, the proceeded to eat it. It was a young gull, but it was bigger than the falcon. Usually the falcons grab their prey in mid-air, hang on with one foot, and double up the claws of the other foot like a fist. [Then they pound] the prey to death. The falcon's feet are very powerful, and usually about three heavy blows are more than enough to kill. They don't just injure the prey and let it get away—they kill instantly, and devour it right away. It was interesting to watch him keep pecking away on the head, till finally his foot was free, then he proceeded to pluck the bird and eat. Dorothy was kneeling down within two feet of him taking pictures, but the bird paid little attention to her. Of course he was watchful, but he didn't make any attempt to go elsewhere. Ruth and Pete were standing further back. It was chilly, but this was too interesting to worry about getting an extra jacket on. The audience finally left when it was getting too dark to see well any more. Falcons have very strong hooked and notched bills, and very large, strong feet with strong sharp claws. Wings are strong and powerful, too. They have very keen eye sight and are very fast in flight. They sometimes reach the speed of 180 to 200 miles per hour, when descending on their prey.

Some of you will feel badly when I tell you this. It's about the cross on Robbin's Island. We call it Robbin's Island, because it used to belong to a forest ranger by that name. Well, anyway, about the middle of the summer the cross disappeared. Whether it was tossed in the brush somewhere, or transferred

to another spot or burned for firewood, I don't know, but Dorothy has a sneaking idea who was behind the mean trick. Most everyone who has ever been to Knife Lake has seen the cross, and knows what it represents. If they don't know, they inquire at Dorothy's. It has been there ever since 1928—over 35 years. [It] was placed there as a memorial to a man who drowned in 1928. His body was never recovered. At that time, they didn't have divers, or other means of retrieving bodies, and no help to speak of. It was always the game wardens who did the dragging. There were very few outboard motors then and very few people in the woods. So dragging was done under difficulties. There were two men in the canoe at the time of the accident. They stuck with the canoe. The man in back was the weaker one, and every few minutes the man in front looked back to see if the other man was all right. Several times he had to go back and help the other man grasp the canoe again. About a hundred feet from shore, the man went under water. The head man was able to pull him to the surface again, and stayed with him a few minutes, and then he went to the front again, and tried to swim the canoe to shore to make recovery quicker. He kept looking back, and his partner said he was O.K. Then a few minutes or seconds later, he looked back again, and this time his partner was gone. He went back, and couldn't see or find any trace of the man. He kept looking and trying to find him, but he couldn't see a trace of him. He was weakening himself, and finally was forced to give up, and try for shore by himself. This was in the spring of the year, just as the ice had gone out, and of course the water was icy cold, and with all the heavy wet woolen clothes they had on, it was a lot of weight to hang on with. Fortunately, the partner made it to shore and immediately passed out. When he came to, he called for help and while waiting for help to come, he tied two sticks together and placed them on the spot closest to the scene of the accident.

About a week after the cross disappeared, Marshall (Chippewa Outfitters of Duluth) had a camping party near the spot, and he offered to make a new cross, and Dorothy was only too glad to have him make one. I hope this one will stay in its place now. Everyone who noticed the cross missing was very peeved about it. It was just as bad as taking a gravestone from someone's grave. Previously people had respected the cross and considered it a part of the country, [but] it seems like people are so destructive now. The wilderness is good for the soul, so why not respect it and all that goes with it!

Last spring when Dorothy was in town for a few days, Gladys and Laurel took her for a ride up the north shore, and two moose ran in front of the car, so Dorothy finally got her close up pictures of moose. The last time she tried to get pictures was on Knife Lake when she saw a moose swimming across the lake. She got real close to them and took pictures. Then a little later, when it was too late, she discovered she had an exposed film in the camera, so she didn't get her moose pictures. She sure was disappointed for she hasn't seen a moose close enough to get a picture for a good many years. It seems like the moose are making a comeback now.

We [Dorothy and I] hope everyone had a very nice holiday season. And we hope you have the nicest year ever in 1965. Right now the trees are so white and heavy with snow it still seems like Christmas. And all this sub-zero weather makes for good ice. Did you know that the coldest recorded temperature in the world is 90 below zero? This was in Verkhoyansk, Soviet Union, though I don't know what year it was. So what have we got to kick about when it gets down to merely 40 and 50 below here? Count your Blessings, I say. Also did you know that the average person, after he has reached the age of sixty, has taken enough steps in his life to encircle the globe five times? I thought everybody used cars these days.

Well, I don't want to take up too much of your time. I would love to sit around and talk some more, but I'm getting hungry, and I'm sure I must be keeping you from dinner. I wouldn't want you to miss that delightful pastime, I have been nibbling along on the flowers now and then while writing this, so I hope I didn't spill any crumbs on the letter. Dorothy and all our bird friends would like to wish you all the health and happiness possible in the New Year, and loads of good luck, good friends, and good cheer. We thank everyone once more for their many kindnesses in the past, God Bless everyone, and thanks for being so patient and listening to all this.

Very Sincerely,
Ruby Hummingbird and
Dorothy

From the perspective of a Billy the Blue Jay . . .

Dear Friends,

December 1965

Gosh, it's been quiet for a long time now—ever since the last of the summer birds went south. They wanted me to go along, but I figured I'd rather stay up here and spend the winter with Dorothy. It's so beautiful up here in winter I just hate to leave. Maybe later on I'll go away for a few weeks, but I assure you I won't go far. Maybe just a couple miles further into the woods.

It seemed to be such a race late this fall to see who would be the last to migrate from Knife Lake—the seagull or Louie the loon. It seems that every year just a very few loons and seagulls remain up until the very last minutes. But I'm sure they left at the same time. I saw them both just the afternoon before the lake froze. The next day there was a crust of ice over most of the lake and I didn't see any sign of them after that, even though the ice broke up again in a couple of days. I guess old Louie knows just the right time to leave. In fact he has to, because he has to have plenty of open water for a take-off. He can't take off from land or a sheet of ice like the seagull and other birds, so, as I say, he has to know when. Sidney Seagull always beats him back in the spring, but as soon as enough ice has melted, Louie comes back. He has lots of fun swimming under the water, and sticking his head up through a hole in the ice. Dorothy was sorry to see them leave, for that meant winter was close at hand. Dorothy likes winter, but she likes the loon too and now

it would be a long time till she would see him again. So I guess us winter birds will have to keep her cheered up till spring.

All bird land went into an up-roar this fall, and feathers and fur flew all over the place for a while. It all started when Bruno and Brunella Bear said they were going to write this year's letter for Dorothy. None of the birds would stand for it. In the first place I don't think Dorothy likes them well enough to let them write. All they think about is stealing. The second place, they would fall asleep on the job, and sleep the rest of the winter. Why, they were both so sleepy when they made the announcements that they yawned and stretched after every other word. And stretching would make them so tired, they would yawn again. It was easy for us birds to lick them. They finally gave up the fight, if you call it a fight; and I really do believe they were walking in their sleep when they left for their den. Whew! We were sure glad to get rid of them. Since we were all gathered together, we held a meeting, and all the guys voted that I should write the letter. I was sure proud, and nervous, too, for I never wrote a letter before, and I'm not sure I can spell. But they all said they would help me out if I got stuck. There are a few people who don't like me, but I try to make up for my bad faults.

I am very bold, and noisy, and at times I even steal birds' eggs, and occasionally young birds, but not near so much as people blame me for. Often people call me a questionable character, and I guess I am. I can't seem to help it, so I suppose it is an inheritance, I am a very beautiful bird, which is a good thing, because it makes people forget sometimes how bad I am. You see, I am a Blue Jay. A Northern Jay, and would you believe it—I am related to the crows, and ravens and magpies. Ugh!

I suppose that is where I got my bad habits. I'm sure that if people knew me and my relatives better, they would forgive us our faults. Since I am related to the crows and magpies, I can't speak too harshly of them, for they have some very good qualities too, so I'll just keep them out of this. I have various names such as Jay, Common Jay, Corn Thief, Nest Robber, Blue Coat, Cop and Robber, and various unprintable names which some people call me. Most of you have met me many times so you should be familiar with my appearance. I am about ten to eleven and a half inches in length, depending on what part of the country I reside in. I am different shades of blue—my back is a smoky or hazy blue; my wings and tail various shades of bright blue; and black bars, and edged in white. My tail is fan-shaped, and my under-parts are dull white. I wear a black necklace about my neck and throat. I have a blue crest on my head, and my face is bluish white. My bill is cone-shaped, medium length, and strong. Both my wife and I look alike, and our kids are similar. We prefer to build our homes in pine woods or forests, but a few of us reside in the suburbs and country and towns. We love to build our homes in cedars if they are available, and we build the nest from five to fifty feet up. It is built loosely and somewhat carelessly, but some Jays are neater than others with their building. The nest is usually in the fork of the tree, and constructed of twigs, either dry or green, and pieces of bark, leaves, weed stems, and lined with strips of bark, grass, pine needles, rags, paper, string, feathers, or most any soft material that is available. There are three to six eggs, buff to greenish or olive color, and speckled with brown. We only have one brood a year, and both my wife and I take part in building the nest, incubating the eggs, and feeding and raising the young. We are both very attentive to our young. Our food consists of insects, various nuts, grains, corn and a small percentage of eggs, and occasionally a very young bird. It is estimated that only one or one and a half percent of our food consists of eggs and young birds. We are sometimes called planters of forests, because we often carry off acorns, beechnuts, and other seeds, and stash them away somewhere, then immediately forget about them till a few years later we see young trees growing in the vicinity of our hiding places. Wherever we are found, it is our permanent residence, except for a few who migrate. If food is plentiful, we'll stick around. Jays are found all over the continent, but each country or part of the country has its own species, and they are colored differently, depending on what part of the country they are found, and they differ in size, too.

We have a teasing nature, and we like to clown, and steal, and we are destructive, and to top it off we have a lot of "cheek" or "gall" or "nerve," or whatever name you prefer. We hide food, and never return for it. We like to mimic other birds. Our favorite practical joke is to mimic the scream of the red shouldered hawk, and scare all the birds around us.

Well, I think I better stop talking about me, and talk about Knife Lake. I hardly know where to start. Guess I'll go back to last winter. It was a long, cold and snowy one. It hit fifty-four below zero at the coldest point, and a long stretch of twenty to forty plus below. We had more snow than we've had for five years or more, but I know a lot of you fellows had a hectic winter, too. Well, we birds managed to keep warm and got enough to eat. We worried about the deer in all that snow, but I think the Winton snowmobile club spent a day or two going here and there, cutting cedar for them. Some looked pretty starved, but most of them pulled through the winter in pretty good shape. The snow was beautiful the way it clung to the trees, and weighted them down, and the porch windows were frosted all winter. The snow is like us birds—sometimes you cuss us and other times you pat us on the back. Last winter the lakes froze several weeks earlier than they did this year, as the month of November was much colder than it was this year. Even December started off pretty mild. But we had so much snow this November that the lakes didn't have much chance to freeze — to freeze good that is. But it is frozen now, and it's nice to know that Dorothy can walk across the lake safely, and get a change of scenery.

On January 10, one of the snowmobile clubs came through Knife Lake and they had a nice slushy trip. It was 35 below zero then, and those who got wet feet were beginning to feel it. Dorothy had a nice warm fire for them to hang and dry out. Also she had plenty of hot soup and coffee which went over pretty good. For a while, all you could see was wet socks hanging over and around the stove, and wet shoes everywhere. After you got used to it, you could manage to dodge them and push the socks aside and find the soup. I wouldn't be surprised if someone found somebody's sock in their soup too. Well, it was a cold ride for the folks as none of the sleds are closed in. There was plenty of nice, fresh air for everybody. But they enjoyed it all.

On February 13, the Babbitt snowmobile club had a "Dorothy Molter" Day, and they hauled a lot of supplies up for Dorothy. Each sled pulled a toboggan behind it, and they all had supplies. Dorothy was surprised, and pleased to see so much. Although she knew they were going to bring up some things,

she never dreamed they would bring so much. It was really wonderful of the men, and Dorothy appreciated it so much. Between getting these supplies up, and getting the ice cut, Dorothy feels that she has a lot to be thankful for. The lake travel was better this time than it was in January.

Snowmobiles are wonderful, but they can be a big headache, too, and an expense. You people who are against the snowmobile don't really know what it is all about. Of course most of you know that there has been much bickering about the use of outboard motors and snowmobiles. You read books and articles and listen to lectures about the wilderness area and it all sounds so romantic—actually some people come into this country expecting to see it filled with Indians. If they do see someone who is an Indian they can't believe it, because he is not wearing feathers. Well, anyhow, these authors and lecturers tell you all the bad things about the things they don't want up here. They never point out the good, and I think they have the most stupid excuses for wanting to ban them, claiming that they spoil the fishing, litter up the country, and spoil the trees, etc. They claim that the outboards leave a wake, and nearly capsize canoes. Well, actually it is the people in the canoe who tip it—they just panic. And for that matter, of all the canoes that come through this country, I've never yet seen or heard of any being capsized by motors. These same people will go out on the lake in the windiest, stormiest weather, and call it fun riding the waves. Well, they are asking for it. Dorothy thinks there should be no objections to the small motors. Just bear in mind that many a life has been helped and saved by a fellow with a motor. It is the folks who just use the motors to horse around that are objectionable. Most folks who use a motor use it simply to get where they are going. You say why don't they paddle? Well, why don't you walk a couple blocks to the drug store instead of jumping in the car and riding? I think the good Lord made this country for everyone to enjoy. There should be no partiality. Maybe there are a lot of people in the woods. Well, what can you expect when it is so highly advertised? If everyone who came up here caught fish, then you might have some reason to complain.

The summer campers do more littering and damage to the woods than snow sleds ever will, but they don't mention these things to the ardent reader. The only difference between the snowmobile litter and the summer litter is that the fellows against sleds go around looking for a litter spot, then take a picture of it and write something to get up your ire. In summer, the Forest Service has men going around cleaning up the dirty campsites. This gives the impression that the campers leave their campsites spotless. Oh, man! Is that ever a false alarm! Now don't take me wrong, for there are just loads and loads of good campers, whether they are paddlers or motorists. It's just too bad though, that we have to suffer for the offenders. There is so much to see in the woods too, but how many of you go any further than your campsite? Very few want to go on the mainland, and this is your best bet to be near nature, especially plant life. The islands are too much trampled down by campers so unless it is an extremely big island, you won't see much plant life. Just go exploring in the bays, swamps and hills and you'd be surprised at all the new things you see.

Oh golly, I'd better be changing the subject before I run out of paper. Don't take us wrong now—Dorothy is just as conservation minded as the rest of you, maybe even more so, but just remember when you vote against anything, use your best judgment, and study out both sides of the story and ask yourself just how many of your heroes have ever been in the woods before. Oh, I know a lot of them have, but I think you will find that the biggest ones behind it all have never been much further than the water cooler in the office without getting in a car or plane to do their traveling. Oh, this letter must sound awful. Maybe that's why I was picked to write it. But I'm only answering questions that people ask Dorothy in the summertime. So now I'll see if I can talk on a more pleasant subject, but first let's have a snack and some coffee.

A few days ago, a wolf walked right by the boathouse. They mostly come at night or early in the morning, so Dorothy doesn't often see them. But when she is out walking, she sees a lot of wildlife—not every day though. The mink and weasel live on the island, and the fox must hang out nearby, for it seems like its here every night. Why don't people see more of them in the summertime? I suppose because the bear is taking up all their time. So many of the campers have never seen a bear up here, well it's not because there are none. They sure are making pests of themselves. Lots of campers are anxious to see a bear but when they do, it's usually too close for comfort. They have really been bad the past few years. They pestered the life out of Dorothy this summer, knocking over iceboxes and raiding them, and tearing tents. They got into a little wooden building that used to be a houseboat, and run off with the whole carton of Hershey bars (30 boxes). She recovered just about half of them before they were damaged. She hoped that he got a good belly ache from them. Well, at least he was pretty clean about it. He must have eaten paper and all because there were very few papers lying around, but there were plenty of strips of wood lying around from the old houseboat.

Dorothy hardly got any sleep most of the summer. Seems like every time she hit the sack, old Bruno would show up. One night he really did scare the pants off a woman, who was staying in one of the cabins. She and her husband came over about one thirty in the morning to tell Dorothy that the bear was raiding their icebox. So Helen and Dorothy went back with them. They saw the overturned icebox but no bear. So they all sat around in the cabin waiting, and drinking coffee, but nothing happened. Finally Dorothy went back to their tent. Just before they got there, Dorothy saw something light on the ground and picked it up. Lo, and behold, it was the woman's panties. Dorothy looked at them envyingly and wished she could wear such a dainty size. A few nights later these people came back again to say the bear was there again. It was not only Bruno, but also Brunella. The bears ran around all summer long with food packed in their bellies, while Helen and Dorothy packed bags under their eyes. It got so they left the light on all night, not that it kept the bear away, but at least they didn't have to fumble around in the dark for shoes or flashlights. Well, Dorothy says that if she never sees another bear it will be too soon.

Everybody at Dorothy's likes blueberry pie, so she has a standing golden rule—"No picky, no eaty" so everyone took turns picking. It was a good year for berries, but Bruno started on them early, even before they were ripe, but Dorothy knew of a few spots she hoped to beat the bear to. There didn't use to be so many bears around, and it was nothing to pick a bushel of berries off just one small island. But now, between the bear, and being trampled by campers, there are not many berries left on the islands. People think they have picked a lot if they get enough for blueberry pancakes. Oh, there are lots of good places to pick, but Dorothy can't take enough time out to go that far away. She didn't even get time to go to town this past summer but that was the bear's fault. As long as he was such a bad egg, she could not leave the island.

Speaking of blueberries, maybe some of you will remember when the train used to come to Ely. There were two coaches, and Lord help the ones who got on the train during blueberry season! They were lucky to find standing room. The coaches were loaded with blueberry pickers—the train would stop between stations to pick up and drop off berry pickers. People boarded the train with wash boilers, five gallon pails, packsacks, and every conceivable large item filled with berries. It seemed like it took for-ever to get from Ely to Duluth. Most people were bored with that slow ride, but to Dorothy, it was always the best part of the trip from Chicago, or all points south. Excuse me a minute while I get up and stretch my wings. There, that's better. How about some more coffee? Help yourself.

Dorothy was rather glad to see the geese fly over. Although it meant cold weather approaching, it also meant that Bruno and his family would be heading for their winter quarters—thank goodness. Or if they were not headed there yet, at least they would be too lazy by this time to get into any more mischief for another year.

Last April, Dorothy's aunt (Cap's sister) passed away, so Dorothy made a quick trip to Pennsylvania for the funeral. It was near ice break-up time so she couldn't be gone long. She flew from Minneapolis to Pittsburgh and made it just in time for the funeral. It was nice flying over Pennsylvania for it is beautiful country. Also, it's nice to be back in Pennsylvania again. Dorothy would have enjoyed the trip more under different circumstances.

We hope everyone had a nice holiday season, and hope the New Year will bring you much happiness and prosperity, with the best of health included. God bless everyone, and thanks, folks, for listening to me.

Oh yes. As most of you know, Lady Bird Johnson was in Ely this summer, and made a short canoe trip. The trip, supposedly, was to cover some of the old voyageur's trails, and give her some background for an historical article which she will write later, and publish in the National Geographic magazine. However, in an interview over the radio after her trip, it appeared like the trip was arranged purposely to snub the outboard motors. You could tell that the answers to questions were prompted, no doubt, by those who oppose motors. All this talk about the quiet and solitude of the woods, the call of the loon, the song of the birds, etc., sounds very good, but how many authors copy this same old line. I wonder how many birds she actually saw and heard. Not many, I'm sure, for I understand that all her campsites and portages were well sprayed with insecticides for her benefit. I, myself, stayed away from those places, for I don't like my nice juicy bugs garnished with these modern fool-proof ideas. She really roughed it! All her campsites were well prepared, well cleaned out, and thoroughly immaculate, with all the comforts of home, including toilets, and I don't mean the Chic Sale kind. She even had a telephone at one place. Do you think she lived on dehydrated foods, and drank lake water while camping out? Guess again. And all those comfort of home—did they paddle and portage them in? These are the people who use motors and planes, and need a guide—not one

guide, but several of the very best, to handle their equipment. So what does she say, quote: "the stillness and peacefulness of the canoe country was spoiled by the sound of a motor on the canoe which the photographers used."? Well, you can't blame her. She only said what she was told to say. If you didn't read all this stuff about peace and quiet in books, you wouldn't think so much about it. Many and many a person has been glad for the sound of a motor, even though they preferred the paddle. There are plenty of places where it is peaceful and quiet. All you have to do is get off the main lakes, and there they are. Like riding in a car on the highway—nobody wants to take the less crowded side roads—too rough. Bye, bye now. Thanks for listening.

Sincerely,
Dorothy and Billy Blue Jay

From the perspective of Baldy the Eagle . . .

Dear Friends, December 1967–68

Greetings to all from my aerie on Knife Lake, where there are only two seasons in a year—that's ten months of winter and two months of cold weather! This is really a switch for me, I'm used to sitting high in a tree, seemingly on top of the world, and now, here I am sitting as Dorothy's personal secretary. Quite a let down, eh? I was supposed to write her letter last year, but somehow we just couldn't get together on it. She went to Chicago for a short time, and when she came back, she couldn't find me. Then when I did show up, she said it was getting too late and she had other things to do. Now, here we are together again, and we'll see what we can do. She has her pot of coffee handy, and I have my rotten fish outside, so I guess we are ready to get started on our letter.

First of all I'll tell you something about myself. I am Baldy, the Bald Eagle, or the American eagle; if you prefer it that way. A few call me the White-headed Eagle. I live on Knife Lake and am a permanent resident there, and I have relatives living all over the woods, but we respect one another, and build our homes three to five miles apart and farther. That way we don't interfere with each other's feeding grounds, and are less likely to run out of food. We are fairly friendly with the ravens and crows, and often join them where there is food handy.

My nest is called an aerie, eyrie, eyrey—whichever way you prefer to spell it, it's all the same. It is built high in a tree, sometimes eighty feet high or more, and most always in a dead tree. We like to make our homes near large bodies of water, and we use the same home year after year, unless our nest is molested. Man and weather, I think, are our only enemies. We repair our nests every year and keep adding to it. Sometimes it gets pretty big and may weigh a ton and more. We make it with big twigs and sticks, and branches which are sometimes two to four inches in diameter; [the nest] is cup-shaped in the center and it is lined with smaller twigs, bark, grass, pine roots, and other small roots.

It is bulky, heavy, and strong, and may be five to eight feet in diameter, and seven feet and more deep—outside measurements. Sometimes the trees break down from the weight, and the wind and snow. Records show a nest that has been used for at least 35 years. Maybe it's still in use, as far as I know. Another nest was found which measured 9½ feet in diameter, and 20 feet deep, and estimated to weigh nearly two tons. It must have been in a very strong tree. Often odd things are found in the nests, like a fish plug, light bulbs, table cloths, large papers, etc. Us eagles mate for life and only if our mates die, do we take on another. Our families are usually two young ones, and sometimes only one. The eggs are a creamy white or maybe you would call it a dirty white, and they are heavily splotched with various shades of brown. Incubation period is about 35 days, or between five and six weeks. My wife does most of the incubating but sometimes I help her, and I bring her plenty of food. When the kids are born, I help feed them, and I bring them more food than my wife does. Boy; are they ever homely! When they are about six weeks old, their wings are so heavily feathered, they can't even lift them, and so they have to wait till they are stronger. They stay in the nest for eleven to twelve weeks before they learn to fly. Us parents don't teach them to fly—they learn by themselves. We simply leave them to themselves, and we go looking for food. We deposit the food not too far away, or hold it at a far enough distance. When the kids are hungry enough, they soon learn to fly after it. The little eaglets grow from about three inches to three feet in three month's time. In a year's time they are as big as I am, and they look more like Golden Eagles, and are often mistaken for them. My wife and I both look alike, but she is a little bit bigger than I am. We average two-and-a-half to three feet long, and have a wing spread of about seven to eight feet. Our plumage is a dull brown over our bodies, but our heads, neck, and tails are pure white. Our bills are yellowish, and hooked, and very strong, and our feet are yellowish, with very strong powerful claws. Our legs are heavily feathered to below the knee joint. Wings are ample and rounded. We use our strong claws to kill prey, and tear it to pieces with our beaks. We have very keen vision, and can spot food several miles away. Our eyes are telescopic and microscopic. The authorities say our eyes weigh more than our brain, and they think we can see one-hundred times better than man. I know I can see much better than Dorothy, because I see her using binoculars to watch the birds. Us eagles are found from Canada to Mexico, and we thrive well in Alaska. Our average life span is thirty years, and we stay in our own nesting places year after year, unless food becomes scarce. Sometimes in winter we leave the site for a brief time when food is hard to find, but we don't go far away. We start repairing our nests in February or March, and start nesting again.

Way back in the year 1782, the Second Continental Congress adopted me as the National Emblem. There was some argument about it at the time, for a lot of people didn't want us eagles to represent their country. Their argument was that we were too cowardly for the part. Ben Franklin wanted the public to vote against us. He impressed upon their minds that we were just plain cowardly thieves and scavengers, and far from noble, and he said other nasty things. He wanted the people to vote for the wild turkey. They said . . . we had a noble and striking appearance, and we had a rather majestic beauty, and a masterful domination of our environment, and stood for power. We won votes. We stand for glory.

Now let's see what I can tell you about Dorothy. I guess you missed her 1966 and 1967 letters. Well, she didn't get any out. She wasn't in the mood to write. As you know, the government forced her to sell out, by condemnation proceedings. That had her down in the dumps for a long time, even though they allowed her to stay until 1975, it still wasn't a very good deal, considering. She had to take the boathouse down by September 1st, and that was a big worry. If the government took it down, she would not be allowed to have the logs, or wood, even for firewood. They would just burn up the works. Well, late in August, her friend, Chuck and his son came, so between them, and Ruth, and Dorothy, they got it pulled down, and Dorothy is still using the lumber and logs for firewood. There is still a lot of cleaning up to do, but she will gradually get it done. It was stupid of them not to allow her to use the wood for firewood, and it was so handy, she wouldn't have to scrounge around for other woods—even in summer it takes wood to keep her warm, and she is always making room for the campers to warm up and dry out. The ways of the government just doesn't make sense. They are just plain wasteful—but I guess that's O.K.—they can just raise the taxes some and make up for it—or try to. Nowhere will you find people more wasteful and more extravagant than the Americans, and the American government. That is a true fact, not just Dorothy's opinion, and if you don't learn that in school, you will learn it when you start making your own living. Oh well, I guess that's their business. Nothing we can do about it except pay our taxes.

We had a rather nice summer for 1967, but it was a short one, and dry. It seemed like it took so long for it to warm up, then there were several weeks of very hot and dry weather, which made the danger of forest fires. There were a number of fires, mostly small ones, but there was a big one in Babbitt—that's right close to Ely. The Canadian side practically closed up till the danger of fire was over. Anyone who did go into Canada had to use Coleman stoves as they were not allowed to build any fires.

During October and early November the deer came to Dorothy's island, but they left before the freeze-up, and returned after the lake froze up, then hung around all winter, and disappeared again in the spring before the break-up. For a time, they could even skate a good part of the way. There wasn't enough snow to use snowshoes. The snowmobile tracks made a good enough trail for the hikers, and made it easy for them to pull their toboggans along behind them, and it was less tiresome than breaking a new snowshoe trail. This has been an unusual year all the way around, and rarely do we get so little snow.

I think the people in Northern Minnesota are pretty lucky weather-wise. Sure, they have extremely cold weather and snow, but they seldom have serious floods, tornados, hurricanes, earthquakes, etc. We have pretty heavy winds and usually a small tornado, or the tail end of one a few times, but compared to other parts of the country, we should count our Blessings. We did get the end of a tornado about the end of April which caused damage enough. Dorothy sat up most of the night reading, and

hearing the trees falling. The trees were so heavy with snow they just snapped in two, if they didn't go over entirely. This was the worst storm since about 1945. Once in a while we have a severe electrical storm. There was one last summer and the lightning struck a little storage building near Dorothy's tent, and splintered it up some but there was no serious damage. Two of her friends from California were here at the time and one man fell down, for no apparent reason, and he felt pretty foolish sitting there on the ground. When the storm was over, Dorothy traced the lightning grooves on the ground, so she thinks that's what knocked him down. Fortunately he was not hurt. Another rut ran right along side her canoe, which was pulled up on shore and turned over. Several trees on the island were struck.

Dorothy was only in Chicago for about ten days last winter. When she came back she went to the Babbitt Winter Carnival. It was their first one, and lasted for three days. It was such a successful affair, I think they plan on having it annually. It was just great, and that's putting it mildly. It started off on a Friday evening with a tremendous basketball game. Both teams were so good one hated to see either one of them lose, but of course someone had to, and it was Babbitt. Since it was such a big event for Babbitt, Dorothy was hoping they would win, especially for this one special occasion. Well you can't say they didn't try, for they sure made a good showing. The game was close all the way through. When one team got behind, first thing we knew, they were way ahead, and so it went, with the result of a tie at the end, which had to be played off. I think it took three rounds to break the tie. I can't think of the word Dorothy wants to use, so I'll let it go as rounds. Dorothy used to be on her school's basketball team. I don't know if the girls have teams any more. I think there was more cheering and noise at that Babbitt game than there was at any world series baseball games. It was terrific! Well, between halves of the game, the queen of Babbitt's first winter carnival was picked, and crowned. And guess who had the honor of crowning her? None other than your friend, and mine—Dorothy. She felt quite honored, and more honored the next night when they held their big dance which they called the Snow Ball. When she walked into the room, the first thing she saw was a huge sign on the wall above the orchestra. She had to blink a few times to believe her eyes. In huge letters on the sign was printed, "Babbitt Welcomes Dorothy." That was a pleasant surprise and if she had her say-so, she would have had the sign read, "Dorothy Welcomes Babbitt." I think most of the population of Babbitt has been to Knife Lake but Dorothy has never been in Babbitt, except once, to see her friends the LaTourells. Well, later in the evening, she was presented with a gift of a beautiful RefrigiWear jacket and hood, and a very nice proclamation from the people of Babbitt, presented by their Mayor. Dorothy is forever grateful for their interest and kindness.

Saturday was the biggest day, with games galore, and oodles of prizes. There were kiddie games, sleigh rides, and snowmobile activities, snow modeling, and all kinds of fun. There was the pancake breakfast where King Kold the 1st was discovered. An unannounced man was in the crowd, and the one who guessed who he was—or rather the one who found him first, won the prize, so every one asked all the men if he was King Kold, till they got the right answer. There was the snowmobile scavenger hunt, too, which was a lot of fun. If you can imagine a man driving a snowmobile with one hand and holding three eggs in the other hand, and trying to get them back to the Country Club without breaking them, you are beginning to get the hang of things. A few of the things they had to bring back were two ice

cream cones, a piece of lemon cream or other cream pie, a paper cup filled with pop—things like that, and a few easier things to carry. They brought one thing at a time, and if anything was broken or spilled, they had to go back for more. Containers to carry the stuff in were barred, so imagine how gooey some of the contestants looked after the hunt was over! There was also a Hobo Supper by the girl scouts which was very nice. Sunday was the fishing contest. It would be nice if a lot of people from the bigger cities could attend these affairs, as it would be a break from their daily grind, and it would be fun for them, too.

The first of May, we had the usual spring storm, and I think we got more snow then, than we did all winter, and Dorothy lost more trees again. It keeps her busy trying to clean up after all the storms. She found a few of the early migrating birds which were either frozen to death or starved to death during the storm. She also discovered the she had a moose on the island one night. She didn't get to see it though. He left his "calling cards" and his tracks.

Due to all the snow and ice, and spring rains, the water was very high this year, and it stayed high. Dorothy went to town one morning, and when she came back that evening, the Carp Lake dam had gone out. Logs were floating all over Birch Lake, near the portage, and Dorothy had to zigzag around them to get to the portage. Then a few days later, the Prairie Portage dam went out. That made it rough for the rest of the summer, and it was bad for the resorts on Moose Lake. A lot of portages all over the woods were under water, and if they were not difficult to find, they were a pretty gooey mess to pack over. Moose Lake was temporarily dammed up to save the water there, and a temporary rollway was put in to make it easier for the travelers to get to Newfound Lake. By late summer the water went down a little and the muddy places dried up some and made portaging a little bit easier. The lakes had dropped six feet, after the Prairie Portage dam went out, and they looked a mess. [Eventually] the Forest Service began working on the dam and I think they got it finished before freeze-up, and they were taking out the makeshift dam on Moose Lake the last time Dorothy was in town, so it looks like travel will go on normally next summer.

Dorothy had her troubles with bears this summer, as usual, but it was more serious. It used to be that she could scare them away, but they refuse to be scared off anymore. So all summer long, Dorothy hardly got a decent night's sleep. Too many bears to chase. She can't have them around because not only the damage they do, but it's too hard for her to get materials up here to repair all the damage, and continuous repairing doesn't keep the bear from starting all over again. The kids keep the premises clean of garbage, so it isn't that which brings them around. They just know that where there are people, there is food around somewhere.

The campers have their troubles, too. Even hanging their packs between trees doesn't help—the bear simply climbs one tree and bites the rope in two and the pack falls in his reach, and believe me, he has a boarding-house reach, which is a long one. Sometimes he drags the entire pack away and it never is found. Then other times he just drags it out of sight and rips it open if it isn't already open, and dumps everything out. He is not choosey what he takes either. Besides the food, sometimes there are other things in the pack to fill in the spaces. Sometimes its sun glasses, cards, mirror, shoes, swim suits, dish towels, soap, etc. Dorothy says that she wouldn't be too surprised some day, to see a bear come out of the woods wearing sun glasses, and a bikini, and admiring himself in a mirror.

One day late in the summer when she thought it might be safe enough to leave for a day, she did go to town and get some supplies. At Carp Portage she met some campers who complained of a bear taking their packsack. They tried to scare him, but he wouldn't scare, so they had to watch him rip the pack, and carry it off. The bear scared them so, they wasted no time breaking up camp. They said he was a mean one, and a big one, too. Other campers had complained previously, about that bear, too.

Dorothy continued on her way, got her supplies, and headed back, hoping she would get over that portage before dark. But she was detained a little, so she didn't have much time to make it. She had five trips across with her stuff, and by the time she made the third trip across, it was quite dark. She took the canoe over first, then a pack and motor and the gas. She put the canoe in the water and put the motor on, then put the packsack in the canoe. Each time she carried something over, she put it in the canoe. The last trip across, she stooped to boost the packsack more comfortably on her shoulder. When she stooped, she got a powerful whiff of a bear, which she had not noticed before. So she hurried as best she could in the dark, but there was no moon yet, and the darkness slowed her up quite a bit, because she was walking over some pretty rocky terrain. She was glad to have this last trip over with. She put the pack in the canoe, and was about to shove off when she noticed that something didn't seem right. She pondered a moment then discovered one pack was missing. She knew she had brought them all across, so it was no use to go back and check. She is always careful to count all her packs, and all the loose stuff she has to carry, so she knew it should be in the canoe. Well, she knew it just had to be the bear—the dirty sneaking so-and-so.

Well, what to do now, in the dark, and without a flashlight. Wouldn't this just have to be one of the few times she forgot it! And which pack was it—the candy pack, food pack or what? She hoped it wasn't the food pack, for it contained so many special goodies. Dorothy doesn't get to town very often, and when she does go, there is always a special pack of special goodies. So, as I said before, what to do now? She hated to give up without even making a try for it, so she did the best she could. There were no campers anywhere near either, so she could expect no help. She knew the bear couldn't be very far away, for he didn't have time to get far. So she suddenly let out a series of her Indian war-whoops, which should have been heard for miles away, and she started throwing rocks around in the bushes, clapped her hands loudly, stamped her feet on anything that would make noise, and banged on the canoe with a paddle. She really made enough noise to wake the dead. She figured she made enough noise to scare him away temporarily, so she could look for the pack. The noise would have scared any of the campers, so why not the bear?

Well, she proceeded to go through the bushes, trying to see ahead. She wasn't going to go too far away, for the pack should be nearby. Her eyes were becoming accustomed to the dark by now, except in the thickets. She had her hand on a bush, ready to shake it. She thought there was a movement, but she didn't see or hear anything. Just the same she had the feeling that she wasn't alone. I suppose most of you have had that feeling at some time or other. Anyhow she stood still, and was on the alert, listening and trying to see around her. To her left appeared to be a trail, so she thought old Bruno might have gone that way. It was no use going any further in the dark, so she decided to come back, and look for the pack in the morning. She saw something white on the ground, and bent over to see if it was

something from the pack. She stood up again and was about to take a step forward when she looked up and heard and saw him. She could have reached out and touched him, he was that close. She stood perfectly still, watching him and ready to make a get-away. He was standing on his hind legs, with his front legs and paws stretched towards her with those awful menacing claws. His mouth was wide open, and she could see every tooth in his mouth, the roof of his mouth, his lulling red tongue, his flaring nostrils. His eyes glowed in the dark like twin flashlights. He was growling and snarling, or whatever it is that bears do. He looked vicious, and just like a dog ready to spring. This was no place for Dorothy to be, but she didn't dare make a movement for the time being, so she just stood still, watching him and ready to make a break for the wide open spaces. She was afraid if she tried to run, the bear would think she was scared and come after her (he would have been right too). He continued to growl and snarl, and Dorothy continued to watch. Then she took a very slow step backward, hardly moving, and hoping she wouldn't stumble on a rock. Then she took another slow step backward, and the growling continued. After the third step back, she turned and walked slowly toward her canoe, hoping he wouldn't follow. If she hurried, she might stumble over the rocks and either get hurt by them, or by the bear—so she was cautious. The canoe wasn't far. She thought if the bear wanted the pack that bad, he could have it. But she wondered what he would do with the mail and her billfold if it was in that pack. Probably round up the other bears, and throw a party.

She reached the canoe O.K. and shoved off, sending back a few last war-whoops for the bear to think about. She was never so glad to have the motor start on the first pull. The next morning, Dorothy sent the boys back to Carp Portage to look for the pack, or what was left of it. She gave them a litter bag to put all the paper, and other litter in that the bear left laying around. They found the pack, just where Dorothy figured it would be. It had been ripped open and one carton of candy was gone. The larger carton was still in the pack, still sealed and untouched. So they brought pack and all home. Although the pack was ripped pretty bad, it wasn't beyond repair. They figured out later that the bear ate over 200 bars of candy. Dorothy didn't know whether to send someone out after the bear with a shot of lead or a shot of insulin. She hopes that bear is in the Happy Hunting Grounds by now, for he was big, mean, and dangerous. If she hadn't known before-hand that the bear was in that vicinity, she would have been far more scared than she was. So she more or less expected to run into him, but she never expected to get that close to him, and she hopes she will never get that close to another one, even in daylight. Half of the campers just laugh and say bears won't hurt you—but just let them run into one once! They don't realize that the bears are becoming more bold each year, and some day someone will get hurt. Most people want to see a bear while they are camping out, but after the bear visits them and does the damage to their tents and packs, they admit they still want to see a bear, but next time they hope it will be far away. Dorothy is always glad when their hibernation time rolls around.

It has been a long slow freeze-up this year. There were no hunters around in Dorothy's area, so I guess they didn't want to take the chance of being "froze in" that far away from the road. No trappers came either.

We hope this finds all of you folks enjoying your winter fun, whatever it might be, and hope you won't be having too much snow to shovel. Also hope you and yours are in good health, and had a nice holiday season. May you have a good winter, and not too cold. Last year it got down to 57 below zero here in the woods, but thank goodness, that is not the daily temperatures—just the coldest part of the winter.

Gee, I think the weatherman is right. We are going to have a blizzard, so if you'll excuse me, I'd better look for a comfy place to sit out the blizzard. This is a long letter, but Dorothy hasn't sent one out for several years, so there was lots to say.

Very best of wishes to everyone, and may you have a healthy and prosperous year. Dorothy wants to thank everybody for the beautiful Christmas cards and letters. When you come up next summer, look for me, or my cousins. Our homes are way up high, in the top of the trees—usually dead trees. But don't get a stiff neck looking up.

All for now, and may God bless you and keep you.

Sincerely, your friends,
Eagle and Dorothy

Conclusion Poem

Dorothy

Small wonder
That the Isle of Pines
Would hold you through the years
A haven in the wilderness
That far few souls can hear.

Where bird song, loons, and moon beams
Glide forever through the trees.
With lifted packs, we tip our hats,
Your living legacy.

J. Oscar Oleson
A gift to the Dorothy
Molter Museum, May 28, 1995

About the Authors

Sarah Guy-Levar has been the Executive Director of the Dorothy Molter Museum in Ely since 2007. When not hauling cases of Dorothy Molter's Isle of Pines Root Beer she enjoys reading, singing, community theater, scrapbooking, camping, dog sledding, entertaining, Tuesday morning breakfast club, and, much like Dorothy, coffee with friends. Sarah resides on Burntside Lake with her husband Andy, daughters Laura and Claire, fourteen sled dogs and one cat.

Terri Schocke began her life in Indiana where she met her husband, Terry. They moved to the Pacific Northwest in 1978, before moving to Ely, MN, in 1997. While living in Ely, Terri has been involved with the Ely Winter Festival, the North American Bear Center and is currently employed at the Dorothy Molter Museum. In addition to photography, a hobby she shares with her husband, she enjoys canoeing the lakes of the BWCA.